More Faith in My Day

Emilie Barnes

HARVEST HOUSE PUBLISHERS

EUGENE, OREGON

Cover by Terry Dugan Design, Minneapolis, Minnesota

MORE FAITH IN MY DAY

Emilie Barnes
Copyright © 2005 by Bob and Emilie Barnes
Published by Harvest House Publishers
Eugene, Oregon 97402
www.harvesthousepublishers.com

Library of Congress Cataloging-in-Publication Data

Barnes, Emilie.
More faith in my day / Emilie Barnes.
   p. cm.
Includes bibliographical references.
ISBN 0-7369-1556-7 (pbk.)
1. Bible. O.T. Proverbs—Devotional literature.   2. Christian women—Prayer-books and devotions—English.   I. Title.
BS1465.54.B37 2005
242'.643—dc22   2004022105

Printed in the United States of America

05 06 07 08 09 10 11 / VP-MS / 10 9 8 7 6 5 4 3 2

This book is dedicated to my wonderful husband, "My Bob." All through our married life of 49 years, he has exhibited the greatest example of a man with wisdom. He has been most wise when it comes to spiritual leadership in our family, our economic decisions, the wholesome raising of our children and grandchildren, and pulling together our marriage in a very special bonding between the two of us.

I am continually going to him for good advice. Bob is able to separate the important from the unimportant. One of the highest compliments he has ever received came from his 20-year-old grandson, Chad. He told Papa Bob this year that he was the wisest man he knows. Bob just beamed with that compliment.

Bob has always tried to be a doer of God's Word. His decisions over these many years is evidence of him living out what the book of Proverbs teaches. Bob is truly a wise man of God's principles for life.

Introduction

*T*he Old Testament book of Proverbs is a wonderful collection of literary thoughts dating back to 950–700 B.C. Though the theme running throughout the book is wisdom for living, the specific teachings include instruction on folly, sin, goodness, wealth, poverty, the tongue, pride, humility, justice, strife, gluttony, love, lust, laziness, friends, the family, life, and death. The book of Proverbs covers it all. Almost every facet of human relationships is mentioned, and the teaching of the book is applicable to all men and women everywhere.

Many proverbs are condensed parables. The sayings in Proverbs form a resource of instruction and teachings on how to live a godly life here on earth and how to be assured of reward in the life to come.

Most of these proverbs were credited to the vast writings of King Solomon. However, a few of them were written by other people—such as Agur, author of chapter 30, and Lemuel of chapter 31.

Since most of these proverbs were written in the masculine voice, I have transferred these thoughts to be applicable to the female gender. A principle is a principle and can be applied to both genders.

Each scripture used from Proverbs is selected because of its teaching on living life on a daily basis. Each proverb relates to the commonness of life as a believer. I have attempted to be very practical in the body of the meditation, writing each devotion as I have lived out God's Word in my life. With each thought, I have given a model prayer that you can use if you are not used to praying. Hopefully, you will eventually be able to pray on your own.

Then there is always an "Action" to reinforce what you have read. Putting your reading into practice helps you learn and apply it. If you cannot put it into action, then there has not been much learning. The final thought is "Today's Wisdom." This thought is to encourage additional ponderance on the particular proverb and devotion. Altogether the package can be a real learning opportunity as you study God's Word on a daily basis.

Another unique feature of this book is that you do not have to start at the beginning and go straight through. You can skip around to find the devotion that speaks to you that day. At the top of each devotion there are three boxes. Put a check mark in one of the boxes each time you read that particular devotion. This way you can keep track of the readings you have previously done.

These short devotions will encourage you to develop a habit of getting into God's Word on a daily basis. Research has shown that if someone does an activity for 21 days in a row, a new habit will be formed.

May God bless you as you seek to add more faith to your day.

□ □ □

Watch Out for Shallow Waters

*My [daughter], if you accept my words and
store up my commands within you...
then you will understand the fear of the
LORD and find the knowledge of God.*

—PROVERBS 2:1,5 NIV

We live in Newport Beach, California, just one block off the Pacific Ocean and Balboa Bay. Each day we have two high tides and two low tides. The thousands of boaters have to be careful that they pay attention to the tide charts. If not, they can have serious problems.

One of the conditions for safe, enjoyable boating is to make sure that the water is deep enough. If the water is too shallow, you run the risk of running aground and breaking out the bottom of your boat. Similarly, spiritual shallowness is not a good condition for our personal lives.

How do we develop a deep walk with the Lord—one that protects us from the shallowness of life? In Proverbs 2:1-9, I have found four provisions that might help you in this "walk with depth":

> ◆ *Saturate your life with the Word*—We are to respond to the Word of God and know it inside and out. "My [daughter], if you accept my words and store up my commands within you... (verse 1 NIV). In this regard, we are to have faith in God's inspiration of Scripture (2 Timothy

7

3:16). If we doubt this inspiration, we will doubt verse after verse, and the Bible will hold no constants for us.

◦❧ *Desire God's Word*—We are to be open to what God is saying to us, and begin to desire what He has for us: "...turning your ear to wisdom and applying your heart to understanding" (verse 2 NIV). This is why a daily habit of being in God's Word is such a valuable discipline. The more we know, the more we fall in love with God's words.

◦❧ *Develop a prayer life*—"If you call out for insight and cry aloud for understanding..." (verse 3 NIV). Every mature Christian whom I have ever met has had a strong devotional life. Our prayer time is when we really get to know who God is, and when He can speak to our heart.

◦❧ *Be consistent in your walk*—"If you look for it as for silver and search for it as for hidden treasure..." (verse 4 NIV). In 1849 gold was discovered in California, and those early prospectors spent years searching for their treasure. They had to be persistent and consistent. That is how it is with our approach to God's Word. There are no overnight miracles when it comes to overcoming the shallowness of life. The race of life is not a sprint, but a marathon.

What will be the result of abiding by these four principles? In verse 5 we read that we will learn "the fear and the knowledge of God." That is a high-tide mark. Our boat will not run aground because of being in shallow water if we fear and know God.

Prayer: *Father God, may my life truly reflect the fear and the knowledge of You. May I stay afloat and not be damaged because of sailing in shallow waters. You are the Commander of my ship. Amen.*

Action: Check your tide tables today. Is there enough water to prevent you from going aground? If not, wait until high tide.

Today's Wisdom:

Knowledge is horizontal. Wisdom is vertical—it comes down from above.

—Billy Graham

☐ ☐ ☐

Have a Thirst for Learning

A wise [woman] will hear and increase learning,
and a [woman] of understanding
will attain wise counsel.

—Proverbs 1:5 NKJV

One evening the grandchildren were over for dinner, and Papa Bob was at his desk working on a manuscript for a new book. As usual he had a stack of reference books piled on top of each other, a paper, and a pen he was using to jot down some notes and references. As the children came upon this scene, one of them stated, "I didn't know that you had to do homework after you graduated from high school." Papa laughed and used the opportunity to talk to the grandchildren about continual learning in life.

Someone once said, "A wise man does in his youth what a foolish man does in his old age." So true! Do not wait until you are old to make wise choices. If you are like most people, you have wasted too much of your life doing and making unwise decisions.

It is funny how we meet some young people who openly assert they know it all and nothing can be taught them. They already, at a young age, know it all. On the other hand, we meet elderly people who cannot get enough learning. One such friend of ours, Mary, is 91 years old. She cleans, shops, drives her own car, and gardens (she even climbs a ladder to prune her fruit trees). In conversation with her it is obvious she still wants to learn. Mary continually asks why and how, and is always stretching her mind to new horizons, never satisfied that she already knows all that life has to offer.

The Hebrew word for *learning* in today's verse means "a taking in." If we desire to grow in our knowledge of God and learn to please Him, we need to be willing to discard old ideas and take in new ones that more adequately give proper understanding to Scripture. People who are seekers welcome new ideas. Are you willing to listen, to be tested, to learn?

Prayer: Father God, let me be open to learning. May I always want to take in new things, and to change my thoughts when new evidence is presented. Amen.

Action: Learn one important new truth today. Share it with someone.

Today's Wisdom:

The more we know, the greater our thirst for knowledge. The water lily, in the midst of waters, opens its leaves and expands its petals at the first pattering of showers, and rejoices in the raindrops with a quicker sympathy than the parched shrub in the shady desert.

—Samuel Taylor Coleridge

☐ ☐ ☐

Make Wise Decisions

*The fear of the LORD is the beginning
of knowledge; fools despise
wisdom and instruction.*

—PROVERBS 1:7

*P*roverbs is about living life in a sensible way. It is about choosing wisely. And the fear of the Lord is the first step toward wisdom. Those who read and practice its principles, who listen to wise instructions, will prosper in the *now* as well as in the future.

I have a tendency to try to put something together without first reading the instructions. However, the older I get, the more I realize how futile this is. I now find myself going to the instructions in an effort to do it right the first time. Going point-by-point and step-by-step makes the construction process so much easier and far less stressful. The same is true with godly principles: Go to the Instructor's manual first before trying to unlock all of life's mysteries.

In several passages of the New Testament, this fear of the Lord is said to be man's proper acknowledgment of who He is (see Luke 12:4-5; Ephesians 5:21). God is always present, and wisdom begins when we acknowledge this fact. In the twenty-first century we can be sure that God is present in man and has gifted all of us with a mind that can respond to Him.

The knowledge that Solomon's wise sayings offer us goes beyond accomplishments. His advice centers on moral responsibility—how to conduct ourselves in various situations in everyday life. His fundamental instruction is to fear and trust the Lord. Solomon challenges us to continually seek God's wisdom in the decisions we make each day.

We must think clearly and spiritually if we are to survive the present cultural war in America. We cannot be swayed by what the secular world says.

Prayer: *Father God, we want to be people who seek after Your knowledge. Teach us Your ways. Amen.*

Action: Search Scripture to answer your basic questions of life. Look to God for your hope, not to the local newscast.

Today's Wisdom:

  When we let Christ become the source of our wisdom, He will guide us in making wise decisions and acting on them.

          —Elaine Creasman

□ □ □

Gated Communities

*But he who listens to me shall live securely and
will be at ease from the dread of evil.*

—PROVERBS 1:33

In Southern California many of the new housing communities are constructed behind fenced-in walls and a guard gate. One of the main considerations in buying a new home is security. In days gone past we could leave our wallet on the front seat of our unlocked car, and the keys in the ignition—but that is no longer true. What has gone wrong? People are saying they do not feel safe anymore. They want that added privacy and security. The past 20 years have certainly made us more insecure about our safety and lives. Even though there are still areas in America where you can leave your homes and cars unlocked, Southern California is not one of them.

However, as Christians we can still know and enjoy the peace of God in this insecure world. A few years ago Bob Mumford, a popular Bible teacher, stated, "Peace with God brings the peace of God. It is a peace that settles our nerves, fills our mind, floods our spirit, and in the midst of the uproar around us, gives us the assurance that everything is all right." This is so true for us who trust in the Lord.

I know from personal experience with cancer that God can give us a peace beyond all human understanding. As I wake each morning, I can be assured that my heavenly Father will be the same that day as the one before. Even though other people might fail me, He will never let me down. I am confident when I approach His throne that I will be in His presence and I will experience His peace. I am never left out. God is never too busy for me. When I pray to Him, He listens.

God has a record of hearing all my prayers and answering them. He has not always responded to them as quickly as I might have liked, and His answers were not always the ones I wanted to hear, but He has never failed to give me the peace that I have needed—and more.

I need to remember that even on those days when God seems far away, His peace is nearby. I do not need a wall and a gate to give me peace. His peace is always available, and it gives me the assurance that everything will be okay.

Prayer: *Father God, may I enter into Your peace today. Let me trust You with my life, my marriage, my family, and my possessions. Amen.*

Action: Lean firmly on Jesus' promise to give you peace.

Today's Wisdom:
               There will be no peace so long as God remains unseated at the conference table.
                                               —William M. Peck

□　□　□

Faith Leads to Understanding

Make your ear attentive to wisdom,
incline your heart to understanding.

—Proverbs 2:2

Throughout Scripture we come across the word *understanding*. I know as a parent that I so desired our children to acknowledge that they understood what I was telling them. No matter how much we listen, if we do not understand what is being said, we have not communicated.

Several years ago Bob and I took a vacation to a wonderful beach resort in Mexico. Naturally, a fine restaurant was in order for one of our balmy evenings. As we entered the facility, we were impressed with the setting, the decor, and the music. It was a perfect place for a memorable evening. Our native waiter came to take our order. After each item ordered he uttered, "Si," as if he understood. When he arrived with our dinner, it was nothing that we had ordered. Even though he had listened to our order, he had not understood anything we said.

That is why we must seek wisdom and then incline our hearts to understanding. We must be careful where we go for information. If we read, see, or listen to the world, we will not gain biblical understanding.

Augustine of Hippo said, "Understanding is the reward of faith." Hebrews 11:1 reads, "Now faith is the substance of things hoped for, the evidence of things not seen" (NKJV). Do you ever have trouble understanding what you had not seen or touched? The disciple Thomas did. He could not bring himself to believe in Jesus' resurrection until he actually saw and touched Jesus. Jesus told Thomas, "Because you have seen me, you have believed; blessed are those who have not seen and yet have believed" (John 20:29 NIV). I do not think that Jesus was scolding Thomas. He was just saying that Thomas would be a lot happier if he could learn to take some things on faith.

Every day I take it on faith that my car will start, my TV will click on, my Internet Web site will function. I do not really understand any of these things. They seem like miracles to me. But they work—at least most of the time! So if I can manage to believe in these man-made miracles, why should I have trouble believing in God? Though I have not physically seen Him, I have felt His presence, I have seen His works: the water, the trees, the mountains, the deserts. All are His creation.

Our faith can bring us to understanding, and understanding can lead us to Jesus and salvation. Let's be receptive to God's wisdom.

Prayer: *Father God, You are so awesome! I can hardly comprehend who You are, but I rely on the Scriptures to tell me all about You. Thank You for letting me understand a little about You. Amen.*

Action: Read 2 Timothy 3:16.

Today's Wisdom:

    Be it ours, when we cannot see the face of God, to trust under the shadow of his wings.

    —Charles H. Spurgeon

☐ ☐ ☐

Keep Your Love Fresh

For the LORD gives wisdom; from His mouth
come knowledge and understanding. He stores
up sound wisdom for the upright; He is a shield
to those who walk in integrity.

—PROVERBS 2:6-7

A few years ago our dear friend Bill was diagnosed with an advanced stage of leukemia. After eighteen months and three rounds of chemotherapy, Bill went home to be with his Lord. Soon after his death when his wife, Carole, was getting ready to visit Bill's sister in San Diego, she decided to take her some of Bill's old books. While sorting through them, Carole found an envelope addressed to her from Bill. He had written Carole an Easter card two years earlier, and she had tucked it away in one of his books. Rediscovering the card, she thanked God for her husband's written words.

Carole had this Easter message from Bill. It read:

> A Tearful week
> A Long week
> A Hard week
> A Lonely week
> A Painful week
> A Revealing week
> A Recovering week

A Reassuring week

A Peaceful week

A Rededication week

A Friendship week

A Love week

A Roller Coaster week

A Renewal week

A Glorious week

A Victorious week

A Life Changing week,

But a week I will never lose sight of.

> May God be our source of true love and friendship. You have been so good these days. I love you for it. You have been all a husband would desire. Forgive me, Sweet, for not keeping our love fresh. I love you. Happy Easter and Happy Beginnings. Bill.

Bill's words offered Carole a comforting sense of his love and presence after he was gone. When Bill was alive, this couple spoke openly of their love for one another. At times the words would grow sparse and far between, but a new season would bring a fresh renewal to their conversation. This was such a time.

As couples we need to learn the language of love. We need to practice saying, "I love you." We need to say these words, but we also need to speak them through our sensitivity to our spouse, our actions, and our conversation. If I am going to run some errands, I can ask Bob if there is anything I can get for him while I am out. My love overflows when I make his favorite food, or volunteer to go with him to his favorite sporting event. Even my choosing to watch an action movie over a love story brings a smile to his face. It does not take much. The little courtesies pay big dividends.

Whenever I choose to show my love, I say to Bob, "Just another way to show my love." Acts of kindness like this are powerful and effective ways to strengthen my friendship with Bob. Such thoughtfulness shows your husband that you do not take him for granted.

Bob and I also rely on certain family rituals and traditions to give us an opportunity to express our love for one another. We kiss each other good night and say, "May God bless your sleep." We celebrate our love on anniversaries and birthdays by giving each other small gifts. We telephone one another when we are apart, visit one of our favorite restaurants on special occasions, go out to lunch, attend the theater, and share hugs. All of these things—spontaneous little acts as well as carefully planned events—are ways to show your mate that you love him. Ephesians 5:21 (NIV) states, "Submit to one another."

One word of caution! Be sure you are expressing your love in the language—in the words and actions—that your spouse will understand as love! Just because you feel loved when he takes you out for a special dinner does not mean that he will feel loved when you do likewise. Be a student of your mate. Know what makes him tick and ticked. Know what best communicates to him the love you have. Keep your eyes open for common, everyday events that give you the chance to express that love.

I continually strive to make sure that our love is patient and kind, that it does not envy, does not boast, and is not proud. It is a lifetime of challenge in developing a Christlike expression of love one to another.

Keep your love fresh. Do not waste the precious days you have. Sunsets do not wait. Do it today.

Prayer: *Father God, I want my husband to know that I love him. Teach me to be more open about my feelings. Help me to be a student of him so that I know what actions and words make him feel loved. Amen.*

Action: Go out for dessert with your husband and share from your heart something that you have been holding inside.

Today's Wisdom:
There is no harvest for the heart alone; the seed of love must be eternally resown.

—Anne Morrow Lindbergh

□ □ □

A Dream with a Deadline

*For wisdom will enter your heart and knowledge
will be pleasant to your soul.*

—Proverbs 2:10

esearch tells us that if we involve our various senses, we will learn and retain more information than if we just think something in our head. Writing down our goals on a sheet of paper gives us greater assurance of actually accomplishing those goals than if we simply think about them. Daydreaming can be fun, but if we do not develop a plan of action, it will remain just daydreaming. Many times those of us who daydream never go on to the next stage of planning how we can effectively implement those dreams.

In my book *More Hours in My Day* I go to great lengths in developing how to write out goals for your life—both short- and long-term goals. A goal is nothing more than a "dream with a deadline." Is not that a great way to think of it? Dreams are wonderful. So are goals. Making them happen is another story. When accomplished they give great personal satisfaction.

Proverbs 29:18 says if we have no vision, we perish (KJV). We are either moving ahead or falling back. There is no middle ground. Remember that goal-setting must include a measurable result and a realistic deadline.

For example, "I would like to lose 15 pounds by June 15" offers both a measurable result and a deadline. But even in goal-setting we should allow ourselves some slack. Goals are not cast in concrete. They just point us in the right direction.

You might want to make a list of the areas of your life where goals are important. These areas could include:

- ∽ physical
- ∽ relational
- ∽ financial
- ∽ professional
- ∽ spiritual

You get the idea! Start setting goals and be sure to make them measurable.

You can make goal-setting a family activity as well. Around the dinner table ask each family member what his or her goal is for the next week, month, or even year. Your children will see how important dreams are and how a family can help one another reach their goals. After this discussion, pray for each person's goal.

It is amazing how just taking the time to physically write down your measurable goals helps you jump-start what you want to accomplish. It is also very rewarding when you are able to check off each activity as completed. *Plan to succeed, not to fail.*

Prayer: *Father God, through faith a dream of eternal life is granted. I ask that You would fill my life with goals that are pleasing to You. May they carry out Your dreams for me and my family. Amen.*

Action: Start a journal if you do not have one. Record your God-given dreams with realistic deadlines. Periodically check your journal to see if you are on track to meet your deadlines.

Today's Wisdom:

Where do you want to go in life? How do you want to get there? Do the roles you fill contribute to your goal? What is really important that you do? What merely fills up time? In determining your best roles, keep those that advance you toward your goal and eliminate those that are useless and a drag. Your trouble may be too many good roles. You cannot afford to take on more than you can handle well.

—Henry R. Brandt

I am the God of the stars.
Lift up thine eyes and see
As far as mortals may
Into eternity!
And stay thy heart on Me.

—AMY CARMICHAEL

Recalling the Past

*My [daughter], do not forget my teaching, but let
your heart keep my commandments.*

—PROVERBS 3:1

*I*sn't it fun to look through old picture albums and recall all the special events of your life? The photograph is truly one of the greatest inventions of all time. Without that little bit of film (and now digital camera memory cards), we would not be able to visually recall the happy events of our life. Photographs help us remember all the holidays, weddings, celebrations, graduations, and every other grand occasion of life.

One way to pass along your love and your values to your children is to pass on special memories to them. When Jenny and Brad, our two children, graduated from high school, I prepared a "This Is Your Life" album for each of them. I bought scrapbooks and decorated the covers, and then I filled them with items from birth announcements to graduation pictures. There were report cards, hand-drawn pictures, invitations, photos of friends, and letters they had written home from camp. Even now they refer to their scrapbooks for names and dates. They entertain their own children with evidence that they, too, were once children! And it provides Jenny and Brad the opportunity to pass along a legacy to the next generation.

If your children are young, now is the time to start gathering such memorabilia. Do not feel that you have to save every finger-painted picture, but certainly hold on to those that reflect their personality, their creative spirit, and their thoughtfulness. Record milestones with keepsakes like ticket stubs and recital programs. In order to keep such a project from becoming a burden by the time your children are graduation age, I would recommend that you add to this book at the end of each year. This makes it a manageable task.

Our family also has one album just to record our annual Christmas picture along with some valuable information about where we spent each Christmas Day, who was there, what traditions were shared, and a summary of the year, giving a few details about the highlights. Each Christmas we bring this album out and put it on the coffee table. The whole family loves to go through the album to remember the past holidays.

One of my favorite verses is Hebrews 13:8, which says, "Jesus Christ is the same yesterday and today and forever" (NIV). His presence in your home is a legacy that never fades.

Prayer: *Father God, the children grow up so fast. I want to remember the many times we laughed and loved as a family. Let the heritage of their faith be evident in their reflections and memories. Amen.*

Action: Once a month take a photo of your children doing something they enjoy.

Today's Wisdom:

Yesterday...
Like mintage spent, is past recall;
Its echo dimmed beyond time's wall.

Tomorrow...
It never promised earthly man,
Nor does it often fit a plan.

Today...
Is gold that covers hills and dell,
And rich are they who use it well.

—Pearl Phillips

Just Pedal

Trust in the LORD with all your heart and lean not
on your own understanding.

—PROVERBS 3:5 NIV

t first I saw God as my observer, my judge, keeping the things I did wrong, so as to know whether I merited heaven or hell when I die. He was out there sort of like the President. I knew He was out there, but I did not really know Him.

But later on when I recognized God, it seemed as though life was rather like a bike ride, but it was a tandem bike, and I noticed that God was in the back helping me pedal.

I do not know just when it was that He suggested we change places, but life has not been the same since. Life without my God, that is. God makes life exciting!

When I had control I knew the way. It was rather boring, but predictable. It was the shortest distance between two points. But when He took the lead, He knew delightful long cuts, up mountains, through rocky places, and at breakneck speeds! It was all I could do to hang on! Even though it looked like madness, He said, "Pedal!"

I worried and was anxious and asked, "Where are you taking me?" He laughed and didn't answer. I started to learn to trust. I forgot my boring life and entered into adventure. And when I'd say "I am scared," He'd lean back and touch my hand.

He took me to people with gifts that I needed—the gifts of healing, acceptance, and joy. They gave me their gifts to take on my journey—our journey, God's and mine. And we were off again. He said, "Give the gifts away. They're extra baggage, too much weight." So I did, to the people we met, and I found that in giving I received, and still our burden was light.

I did not trust Him in control of my life at first. I thought He'd wreck it. But He knows bike secrets. He knows how to make it bend to take sharp corners, jump to clear high rocks, fly to shorten scary passages.

And I am learning to shut up and pedal in the strangest places, and I am beginning to enjoy the view and the cool breeze on my face with my delightful constant companion, my God.

And when I am sure I just cannot do any more, He smiles and says, "Pedal."

—Source Unknown

When some people say, "Oh, life is so boring. I do not even want to get up in the morning," Bob and I cannot comprehend that kind of comment. We find life so exciting that our feet bound out of bed each day anticipating what God has in store for us.

Each day is a real adventure. Many days God just says, "Come along and trust Me." It would be nice to know every detail, what lies beyond each ridge, and what is around each of the corners of life, but God very patiently says, "Just trust Me. You do the pedaling, and I'll do the leading." Our reply is often, "Are You sure You know the way? What if You make a mistake with my life? But, God, I have never been this way before. What if..." The dialogue can go on for hours, days, and months, but eventually we arrive at the point where we say, "God, You lead and I'll keep on pedaling."

As our key verse says today, we are to trust in the Lord with all our heart and not lean on our own understanding. That is so hard to do if we are not used to turning over our lives to Someone who is bigger than us. Just relax and let God be all that He says He is—*trustworthy*.[1]

Prayer: *Father God, You know how hard it is for us to let go and let God. We human beings are so used to being in control. We have a very difficult time trusting anyone else, especially Someone we cannot even see and touch. Please stay close to us when we doubt. It is not that we do not want to trust, it is just that this is so new to us. Please be patient with our little steps, for one day we will be able to run and not stumble. But today we feel like young children who are just beginning to crawl. Amen.*

Action: List in your journal four things that have been bothering you and that you want to give to God. Share these things with your spouse. Pray together about them. Trust God!

Today's Wisdom:

     Faith never knows where it is being led, but it loves and knows the One who is leading.

                                —Oswald Chambers

Acknowledge Him Today

In all your ways acknowledge Him,
and He will make your paths straight.

—Proverbs 3:6

*D*o you have the type of home where nothing seems to get done, where each room would take a bulldozer just to clean up the mess? You rush around all day, never completing any one job. Or if you do complete a task, there is a little child behind you, messing everything up again! There is not one of us who has *not* experienced these feelings.

When I was 20, our baby daughter, Jennifer, was six months old. We then took in my brother's three children, and within a few months I became pregnant. With the subsequent birth of Brad, that gave Bob and me five children under five years old. My life was work, work, work, and yet I never seemed to get anywhere. I was running on a treadmill that never stopped and never moved ahead. I was always tired and never seemed to get enough done, let alone get enough sleep. I was fragmented, totally confused, and stressed.

Then one day during my rushed quiet time with the Lord, I read Proverbs 3:6: "In all your ways acknowledge Him, and He will make your paths straight." I fell to my knees and prayed,

> Please, God, direct my path. I acknowledge
> You to help me, Lord. I am going to allow You

to lead me and not lead myself in my power. I
want Your power and direction. Lord, I am tired.
I am on overload with husband, home, children,
and meals. I have no time left over for me or
anyone else. I cannot even do any of us justice.
Please help me to put it all together and make
it work to glorify You and Your children. Amen.

The Lord not only heard my prayer that day, but He
honored it as well. I began a program that changed my life.
I committed 15 minutes (at least) per day to my quiet time
with the Lord. I got up earlier each morning. The house was
quiet, and my Lord and I talked as I read His Word and
prayed.

Next I committed 15 minutes each day to the organization of our home, concentrating on things I never seemed
to get done: the silverware drawer, refrigerator, hall closets,
photos, bookshelves, piles of papers. I committed to this
for 30 days, and the pattern was set. God was directing my
path. Our home changed dramatically. The cloud of homemaking stress lifted, and I had new direction. The Lord
redeemed my time with Him. I had more time to plan
meals, make new recipes, play with the children, take walks
to the park, even catch a nap from time to time.

Looking back now as a grandparent, I can truly understand the meaning of acknowledging Him in all my ways.
It is looking to God for help and comfort in *all* the ways of
our life: our families, home, finances, commitments, and
careers. God gives us a promise: "I will direct your path."[2]

Prayers: *Father God, sometimes I feel my life is truly on
overload. There are days I am confused, frus-
trated, and misdirected. I come to You on my
knees, seeking Your undying patience and the
hope You so graciously give. I ask for Your direction in my life. Make order out of disorder. Thank
You! Amen.*

Action: Spend time with God today.

Today's Wisdom:

Man's ultimate destiny depends not on whether he can learn new lessons or make new discoveries and conquests, but on his acceptance of the lesson taught him two thousand years ago.

—Rockefeller Center

□　□　□

Good Health Pays Dividends

*Do not be wise in your own eyes; fear the LORD
and turn away from evil. It will be healing to your
body and refreshment to your bones.*

—PROVERBS 3:7-8

Have you ever said after a hearty dinner, "I am so stuffed that I could die"? We all have at one time or another, but for many Americans that is the rule rather than the exception. When Bob and I go to a buffet (which is seldom), I am amazed at the amount of food that is placed on a plate and how many times that plate goes back for more. When dessert time comes, one piece of pie is not enough. We have to have a pie, a cookie, an ice-cream sundae, and a delicious-looking fruit tart with whipped cream. Then, of course, there is a carbonated drink that is refilled (free of charge) two to three times.

No wonder we are a country with a high percentage of overweight people with poor health and a likely future diagnosis of diabetes. All of this adds potential cost to our health-care system, not counting the loss of productive time due to us being off work sick.

Our body is one of God's most precious gifts to us, believe it or not! Each of us has the responsibility to understand how his or her body functions and to work (which takes effort) to take care of it. If you have been a little lax in this regard lately, I hope these tips help in getting you back on track.

Always select single-serving sizes of snacks and desserts to help prevent yourself from eating too-large portions. Refrain from talking while you eat. It is all too easy to down a lot of food without realizing it. At parties, survey the buffet and decide on two or three items—maximum.

Always remove the skin from poultry. You will automatically reduce the calories in it by about 25 percent. Put your salad dressing in a small spray bottle and mist your salad. You will get the taste without a lot of calories. Be sure to add healthy servings of fruits and vegetables to your daily meals. Remember, the darker green lettuce is the healthier for you.

Reduce the amount of caffeine and carbonated drinks that you consume. Instead, substitute club soda and decaffeinated drinks. Increase the amount of water you drink each day. Most of our bodies are dehydrated and need more water. If you wait to drink until you are thirsty, you have waited too long.

Recent studies reveal that most Americans do not get enough sleep each day. Plan on getting a minimum of eight good hours daily. If your job or routine permits, try to get a 15- to 20-minute catnap each afternoon.

Get active. Walk each day, join a health club, have some exercises you can do at home or the office. The older you get, the more exercise you need. Today, the wrong people exercise. The young ones exercise the most, and they do not need it as much as the older citizens.

Good health makes good sense.

Prayer: *Father God, please help me to discipline myself to exercise. Help me to say no to one more serving of dessert. Amen.*

Action: Check out membership to a health club and join it.

Today's Wisdom:

The good and the wise lead quiet lives.

—Euripides

When God is Absent,
all sorrows are here;
When God is Present
all blessings are mine.

—A QUAKER PRAYER

Finding God in All the Right Places

*How blessed is the [woman] who finds wisdom
and the [woman] who gains understanding.
For [wisdom's] profit is better than the profit
of silver and her gain than fine gold.*

—Proverbs 3:13-14

I guess all of us would like to find a pile of silver or gold. Often we look for it in the wrong places. We look at the lottery, and it is not there. We look at a quick scam, and it is not there. We look at gambling, and it is not there. Someone once told me, "If it sounds too good to be true, it probably is—stay away from it."

However, there are ways we can turn the ordinary into silver and gold. One of those ways is to apply wisdom when we shop. If you are like me, when you stop at the mall to just "browse," you most likely will end up buying something you do not need. I have learned that if I am not looking for a specific item, I should stay out of the store. If you want to save money, stop spending money!

Another way to save money is to learn how to decorate inexpensively. Here are a few tips. First, check out your grandmother's attic or your neighbor's garage. (Be sure to get permission first!) If you see something you think you might use, it never hurts to ask if they are willing to part with it.

Garage sales, swap meets, flea markets, and estate sales are great resources for decorating gems. You can take advantage of these opportunities by having measurements of rooms or open spaces written on an index card. Make a list of items you would like to find so you can stick to priorities. In other words, shop with a purpose. If you see a pricey item at an antique store or flea market, keep checking back for a possible markdown, and be sure to express your offer each time.

A professional decorator told me that at least 25 percent of your furnishings should feature quality materials. A beautiful chair or an art print will balance your discount-store linens or junk-shop mirror. Old and new blend together with great grace. It is the secret to decorating beautifully on a budget!

Try not to be an impulse buyer. By acting impulsively, you tend to not be objective about your possible purchase. However, if you run across a once-in-a-lifetime item, you do not want it to slip away.

Prayer: *Father God, You know I want to gain wisdom and understanding. Help me apply these virtues as I go out in the marketplace to shop. I want to be a wise consumer! Amen.*

Action: Invite neighbors over to tea and use only antique cups and saucers.

Today's Wisdom:

The real measure of our wealth is how much we'd be worth if we lost all our money.

—John Henry Jowett

Home Is a Place for Peace

Her [wisdom] ways are pleasant ways
and all her paths are peace.

—Proverbs 3:17

ometimes we become stressed because our home is not the way we want it to be. It lacks something, but we are not exactly sure what it is. Help! What can we do?

Go stand in the center of the room in your house that causes you the most displeasure. This is a fun exercise. There you are in the middle of a room, wondering what to do to make it look attractive. Where do you start? I will be your decorator coach. Let's go.

Build from the basics—the furnishings and their arrangements. Then pretend you are a guest. What is working? What is pleasing to the eye? For example, try keeping a clear visual line from the entryway to the seating areas. Even chairs grouped around a fireplace can be angled so they appear to invite visitors over. And remember, color is one of the easiest—and most inexpensive—ways to unify a room. Try to fill in the blanks with accessories: pillows, baskets, and candles.

Chances are that you sometimes entertain guests with children the same age as yours. Your home is probably already child-friendly for that age group, but I suggest going beyond just child-friendly. Make your home child-inviting. Children respond to feeling welcome, too. Do you have pretty, welcoming things at their eye level?

I have a box of toys, blocks, stuffed animals, and games in a box under our guest bedroom's bed. It can be pulled out at a moment's notice to assist in directing young guests' energy to a constructive beat. Anticipate and always be ready for the unexpected.

Prayer: *Father God, who will enter my home needing comfort? Who needs a place of welcome and refuge? Let me see clearly how I can invite them into Your love. Amen.*

Action: Change the colors in your home with simple additions like candles, tablecloths, and rugs.

Today's Wisdom:

What Is a Home?

A roof to keep out the rain. Four walls to keep out the wind. Floors to keep out the cold. Yes, but home is more than that. It is the laugh of a baby, the song of a mother, the strength of a father. Warmth of loving hearts, light from happy eyes, kindness, loyalty, comradeship. Home is first school and first church for young ones, where they learn what is right, what is good, and what is kind. Where they go for comfort when they are hurt or sick. Where joy is shared and sorrow eased. Where fathers and mothers are respected and loved. Where children are wanted. Where the simplest food is good enough for kings because it is earned. Where money is not so important as lovingkindness. Where even the teakettle sings from happiness. That is home. God bless it.

—Ernestine Schuman-Heink

Sleep Without Fear

*When you lie down, you will not be afraid; when
you lie down, your sleep will be sweet. Have no fear
of sudden disaster or of the ruin that overtakes the
wicked, for the LORD will be your confidence and
will keep your foot from being snared.*

—PROVERBS 3:24-26

Do you ever have trouble sleeping? Then claim the
above promise. I know there can be plenty of nights that
you might toss and turn. You just cannot relax from thinking
about tomorrow's schedule. You have got to do this and you
have got to do that. When will it end? All the tests, one specialist after another, a change of medication—I cannot seem
to keep track of it all. Is it taken in the morning, at noon, at
dinner, or just before I go to bed? Wow! There is a lot to be
concerned about. However, this verse tells me that I can lie
down without fear and even have pleasant dreams.

You do not have to count sheep to fall asleep. Just
remember that God knows all about your tomorrows. He
has gone ahead of you to smooth out the rough patches. No
information from any test comes to you first. He has already
heard and approved of it before you are told. If He takes
care of you today, He will certainly take care of you
tomorrow. Lay your head on the pillow and know He will
protect you from all harm. Night-night![3]

Now that I am back on track after my cancer treatments
and have been able to reduce my medications and doctor

appointments, I find that God's peace causes me to sleep without the worries and tossing and turning in my sleep. Truly there is a comfort and soothing of the spirit so I can fall asleep easily. Each night as I lay my head on the pillow, I close the day off with, "Thank You, Jesus, for another good day. Give me a full night's sleep." Truly, He gives me the desires of my heart.

Prayer: *Father God, I want to be content with whatever You choose to provide. Give me the grace to let the rest of the world go by and trust You for my every need. Amen.*

Action: Trust the Lord that you will have pleasant sleep and that you will enjoy your dreams.

Today's Wisdom:

He has not promised we will never feel lonely
But He has promised that in Him we will never
     be alone.

He has not promised that we will be free from
     pain and sorrow,
But He has promised He will be our help, our
     strength, our everlasting peace.

No matter what happens in our lives, we can
     believe fully in His promise....
We can rest confidently in His love.

—Author Unknown

Living a Righteous Life

*The curse of the L*ORD *is on the house of the wicked,*
but He blesses the dwelling of the righteous.

—PROVERBS 3:33

What a great promise to realize that my home is going to be blessed because I have chosen to live a righteous life!

God is the Creator, and He is still in the business of creating today. Let His creativity shine through you as you create your home. It is really a lot easier than you think to add creative touches here and there as you allow Him to show you the way.

Who would have thought that a bedsheet could be used in so many ways? The first time I used a bedsheet as a tablecloth, everyone thought it was a little strange. Today, however, sheets are used for curtains, drapes, sofa cushions, wallpaper, and much, much more. A friend of mine took Ralph Lauren sheets she bought on sale and decorated her entire house in the same print—a beautiful blue floral. She even put the fabric in her kitchen drawers. The effect was very attractive. All of her friends say, "How creative!"

With a spirit of creativity you can put together a homey environment out of whatever you have. Remember, the key is to keep it simple. You do not have to do all your decorating in one time period. Do one room, then move to the next. This way you will not have the whole house in disarray. When you do it this way, you greatly reduce the stress level in your life.

Proverbs tells us that a woman's worth is far above jewels. Each of us can find sources of creativity as we trust the Creator to enable us and to give us the courage to step out.

Prayer: *Father God, may righteousness be the first ingredient of my godly home. May my life be a living sacrifice to You. Amen.*

Action: Put a note on the bathroom mirror that will make your loved one smile.

Today's Wisdom:

There is no spectacle on earth more appealing than that of a beautiful woman in the act of cooking dinner for someone she loves.

—Thomas Wolfe

The Greatest Prize of All

🌰

With all your acquiring, get understanding.

—PROVERBS 4:7

few years ago, actor Kirk Douglas wrote his autobiography and called it *The Son of the Ragman.* In it he talks about his growing-up years with parents who had immigrated from Russia. He recalls that his mother was warm and supportive and did her best to adjust to a new country, but he remembers his father as stern, untrusting, strict, and cold. Unaccustomed to giving words of encouragement, a pat on the back, or a hug, his father remained a very distant and very private man. But then Douglas shares the story of a special day in his life.

One evening at school, the young Kirk Douglas had a major role speaking, dancing, and singing in a play. He knew his mother would be there, but seriously doubted that his father would go. To his amazement and surprise, about halfway through the program, he caught view of his father standing in the back of the auditorium.

After completing the evening's program, he wanted his father to come up and congratulate him for a job well done, but true to fashion, his father was not able to say much. Instead, he asked his young son if he would like to stop and get a five-cent ice-cream cone. As Kirk Douglas reflects back over all his awards in life, he prizes that five-cent ice-cream cone even more than his Oscar.

As parents, we do not always realize the important role we play in the lives of our families. Our children hunger for our approval. They want and need to know beyond a shadow of doubt that we love them and care about what is going on in their lives. Our kids need our words, but they also need our presence. They need us to spend time with them. Sometimes giving our time says what our words cannot or do not.

In today's verse, God calls us to acquire understanding, and I challenge you to work on understanding your children better. Do not assume you already know what they are thinking and feeling. Let them tell you, and then be ready to laugh when they laugh and cry when they cry. Be a parent they know really cares about the small and the big events in their lives.[4]

Prayer: *Father God, let me have a humble heart so I realize that I do not know everything about the individuals of my family. May my heart continue to search for wisdom and understanding. Amen.*

Action: Take your whole family out tonight for an ice-cream cone.

Today's Wisdom:

My message has been very simple. To live well we must have a faith fit to live by, a self fit to live with, and a work fit to live for—something to which we can give ourselves and thus get ourselves off our hands. We cannot tell what may happen to us in the strange medley of life. But we can decide what happens in us—how we can take it, what we do with it—and that is what really counts in the end. How to take the raw stuff of life and make it a thing of worth and beauty—that is the test of living. Life is an adventure of faith, if we are to be victors over it, not victims of it. Faith in the God above us, faith in the little infinite soul within us, faith in life and in our fellow souls—without faith, the plus quality, we cannot really live.

—Joseph Fort Newton

*Nothing is impossible
when you put your trust in God.*

—EUGENE CLARK

☐ ☐ ☐

Study Each Child

Hear, O my [daughter], and receive my sayings;
and the years of thy life shall be many....Take fast
hold of instruction; let her [wisdom] not go; keep
her [wisdom]; for she [wisdom] is thy life.

—PROVERBS 4:10,13 KJV

The book of Proverbs is full of wonderful sayings that pack a lot of wisdom in a few words. Many of these sayings are familiar. Some you have seen on plaques, plates, glassware, etc. These all contain divine wisdom for the reader. All we have to do is recognize the gems that are embedded in each line. Even though many of the verses are written from the masculine point of view, they are also appropriate for the female gender. Just because a proverb refers to "man," "father," "son," do not ignore the wisdom just because you are a woman. The universal wisdom is appropriate for all.

A wise parent will meditate on each passage in Proverbs and seek out what is being revealed. Today's verse is that way. When Bob and I were raising our children, Jenny and Brad (and we are now helping to influence our five grand-children), we saw many differences between them. We soon came to realize that each child and grandchild has his or her own unique bent, and that this was already established when God placed each child in our family.

God has given you unique children as well. Get to know them. Write down in your journal the ways your children and/or grandchildren are different. Take time to think through the way your training will differ from child to child based upon each one's temperament, life experiences, and even position in the family.

Learn one new thing about each of your children and grandchildren today. Then take this insight and use it to encourage, correct, or instruct. Find a quiet moment to share a specific memory or event with each child. On special occasions we have each child go through our photo albums just to review those events that have helped form that child into the person he or she is today.

The important thing is to praise your child today for being uniquely made. Proverbs 22:6 (NIV) says it ever so simply: "Train a child in the way he should go, and when he is old he will not turn from it."

We know from the field of psychology that married people live longer and happier lives than people who are not married. There must be something in being married that gives the people involved in this arrangement a longer life. When we apply biblical principles to our lives, we certainly do have more purpose and meaning, which gives us a richer life.

Prayer: *Father God, help me not to force all my children into the same mold. Let me take the time to study each of those precious children You have given me. I thank You for trusting me with Your precious belongings. Amen.*

Action: Study your children while they sleep.

Today's Wisdom:

When God wants a great work done in the world or a great wrong righted, he goes about it in a very unusual way. He does not stir up his earth-quakes or send forth his thunderbolts. Instead, he has a helpless baby born, perhaps in a simple home and of some obscure mother. And then God puts the idea into the mother's heart, and she puts it into the baby's mind. And then God waits. The greatest forces in the world are not the earthquakes and the thunderbolts. The greatest forces in the world are babies.

—E. T. Sullivan

Even though I walk through
the valley of the shadow of death,
I fear no evil,
for You are with me.

—Psalm 23:4

Take the Right Fork

Do not enter the path of the wicked, and do not proceed in the way of evil men. Avoid it, do not pass by it; turn away from it and pass on.

—PROVERBS 4:14-15

ow many of us read of an evil deed someone commits and say something like, "How stupid! What was he thinking? He did that for just a few seconds of excitement." We read of these events, and we cannot believe what we read. That evil act will cost the person his family, profession, home, and reputation. He will forever become a marked person.

We think we would never do that. Do not be so confident. At any given moment, we are capable of committing the biggest, darkest sin imaginable! In Romans 12:2 Paul states, "Do not be conformed to this world, but be transformed by the renewing of your mind, so that you may prove what the will of God is, that which is good and acceptable and perfect." The world's system can draw us in very quietly, without making a sound. Seldom do we go from saint to sinner instantly. We gradually give in to our evil desires a little at a time. Then when we are weak, we are easily attracted to doing something we should not do. Satan just prowls around looking for someone to destroy.

All of us are continually struggling with temptations in our lives. The ugly hands of sin reach out to grasp away from us any goodness we may have. We often make smaller and easier choices toward evil before we finally give in to temptation. We must be aware of and sensitive to taking that first compromising step when we face such temptation.

Immediately we must flee from the situation. We must not even enter the path. We must avoid it, pass it by, and walk on. We have to prepare our escape before the event happens. It takes strong, sometimes superhuman, discipline to flee. Rehearse your response to temptation in your mind before you are trapped.

One way to flee is to go to Scripture and read what instruction is given. In Philippians 4:8 we get the following directive: "Finally, brethren, whatever is true, whatever is honorable, whatever is right, whatever is pure, whatever is lovely, whatever is of good repute, if there is any excellence, and if anything worthy of praise, dwell on these things."

Prayer: *Father God, give me clear discernment when I come to a fork in the road. Let me stop and see what Your Word has to say about my situation. Help me turn toward Your righteousness. Amen.*

Action: Keep to the right when you come to the fork in the road.

Today's Wisdom:

Several artists were asked to illustrate their concepts of temptation. When their paintings were unveiled, some of them depicted man's attempt to achieve fame and fortune at any cost, while others pictured mankind's struggle against the alluring desires of the flesh. The prize-winning canvas, however, portrayed a pastoral scene in which a man was walking along a quiet country lane among inviting shade trees and lovely wild flowers. In the distance the way divided into two roads, the one leading to the right, the other to the left. The artist was seeking to convey the thought that sin's allurements are extremely subtle at first—just an innocent-looking fork in the road!

—Author Unknown

Every Day Is a Gift from God

But the path of the righteous is like the light of
dawn, that shines brighter until the full day.

—PROVERBS 4:18

Often when I get out of bed and see that the Lord
has given me another day to rejoice I say, "This is the day
which God hath made; let us rejoice and be glad in it." Truly
every day is a gift from our Lord.

I can remember my eighth-grade English teacher. She
was the hardest teacher I ever had, but I also learned the
most from her. She always was challenging her students to
excel in everything in life. She felt that if something was
worth doing, it was worth doing well. She often gave us
homework assignments which related to interviewing older
people to see what wisdom they could pass on to the next
generation. One such assignment was to ask this question:
"If this were your last day on earth, how would you spend
it?" What a wonderful question! I have often wondered how
I would answer if I were asked that same question. Many
years ago our publisher, Harvest House, had a fine writer
by the name of June Masters Bacher. I had the opportunity
to speak to her on many occasions. She was a teacher and
a fine communicator. In one of her last books before she
passed away, she wrote the answer to this same question.

I would like to share it with you, because it made such an impression upon me:

> I should wear a morning-face, so I could watch earth's full rotation from dawn to wherever day and night meet in twilight. I should rest, reliving other days filled with God's blessings: friends...old hymns...porches...children's laughter....I should watch narrow sunbeams turn windows gold, blind the eyes of sleepy pigeons and filter through the cobwebs. I should listen for the mockingbirds that know all earth-songs and a few of heaven's, too. I should watch the earth drowse at noon when even the sun seems to pause...but I should not sleep lest I miss the building of white cloud-cathedrals and their fall when the thunder-organ sounds. And in the hush that follows a storm, I should look at the washed sky, filled with a million invisible stars, waiting for the night. I should look upon rain-washed hills, mute like the stars, with strength lying their silence....Then happily, I should watch the golden disk sink in the west, leaving me the molten silver of a day well spent, while, like the energy of the stars, never spent at all....And I should hope to take my memories with me. In nothing else am I rich...in nothing else could I be poor.[5]

Here was a woman who truly understood all of God's marvelous creation. She had learned over a lifetime to view the whole creation—not just the sunrises and sunsets, but all that was in between. Cannot you just visualize all that she saw during this last day? Truly she knew that this is the day that the Lord had made, and she was able to rejoice in it.

Prayer: Father God, let me never forget that each day is
a gift from You. I want to appreciate and be
thankful for every minute You give me. Life is
so precious, and I want to enjoy it 24/7. Amen.

Action: Go outside today and take in all that God has
created.

Today's Wisdom:

It was inevitable, I suppose, that in the garden
I should begin, at long last, to ask myself what
lay behind all this beauty. When guests were
gone and I had the flowers to myself, I was so
happy that I wondered why at the same time I
was haunted by a sense of emptiness. It was as
though I wanted to thank somebody, but had
nobody to thank; which is another way of saying
that I felt the need for worship. That is, perhaps,
the kindliest way in which a man may come to
his god. There is an interminable literature on the
origins of the religious impulse, but to me it is
simpler than that. It is summed up in the image
of a man at sundown, watching the crimson
flowering of the sky and saying—to somebody—
"Thank you."

—Beverly Nichols

Have a Prayer Closet

*Do not let them [a father's words] depart
from your sight; keep them [a father's words]
in the midst of your heart. For they are life to those
who find them and health to all their body.*

—PROVERBS 4:21-22

Make a daily practice of reading God's Word and praying. The time of day or location does not matter. Jesus prayed at various times and various places. Your desire to read and pray is what counts. I have realized that God gives me life and health as I open my heart to His Word. During my battle with cancer, I learned that there is something about an illness that makes God's words so very precious. His thoughts are so much higher than our thoughts, and His ways are so much higher than our ways. Use this time to get to know Him in a way you have never known Him before.

There have been times where I was so sick I could not read the Scriptures. Those were the days when my Bob would read to me from the Psalms. What special memories I have of those occasions. They were sweet as honey.

While we were in Seattle receiving my bone-marrow transplant, we would write down comforting words from the book of Psalms on 3" x 5" cards and slip them under the doors of fellow patients. Several times we were caught while delivering these words of encouragement. Each time the recipient said, "Do not stop giving these cards to us. They are so comforting and encouraging."

When we returned home from Seattle and I was able to write again, I made these psalms come alive in one of my new books: *Strength for Today and Bright Hope for Tomorrow,* published by Harvest House Publishers.

Now that I am up and about, I have a special prayer closet where I go each day to spend precious time praying, reading, and meditating on His Word.

Prayer: *Father God, give me the desire to come to You each day and read a portion of Your Word. It will bring healing to my body. Amen.*

Action: Start today to read God's Word. Start with the book of John, and then enjoy portions of Psalms.

Today's Wisdom:

He who every morning plans the transactions of the day and follows out the plan carries a thread that will guide him through the labyrinth of the most busy life....But where no plan is laid... chaos will soon reign.

—Victor Hugo

The Image in the Mirror

*Above all else, guard your heart, for it is the
wellspring of life. Put away perversity from your
mouth; keep corrupt talk far from your lips.*

—PROVERBS 4:23-24 NIV

never thought I would be an older woman,
but my mirror says that I am. Some mornings I say, "Who
is that?" Not one of us cherishes the idea of growing older
and watching our children leave home, seeing our own body
change into something quite different from what it used to
be, and then discovering that, one by one, beloved friends
and family are slipping into eternity. When I was younger,
I always cringed when I read the verse in Titus 2:4, urging
older women to "train the younger women to love their husbands and children" (NIV). Not that I did not want to love
my husband and children, but I did not want to ever be one
of those older women.

Today I consider it a privilege to be an older woman.
In fact, I have a very good friend in Arizona who prays that
she will be prematurely gray so other people will consider
her to be an older woman. I have come to realize how precious it is to have lived life, to have gained some perspective that enable me to share life truths with other women
my age and younger.

One of the most important truths I have found is this:
You can never change another person. But God can. I have
also discovered that the change usually begins with me.

When I begin to change, the other person also begins to change. Remember, when you point a finger at someone, four fingers point back at you.

Be an "older woman" to someone this week. Encourage her to love her husband and family. Encourage her to pray that she would nurture a teachable spirit within herself.

Prayer: *Father God, what a privilege to grow older—to live life to the fullest. In these latter days, make me a fountain of blessing to those around me. I so look forward to being with You someday. Amen.*

Action: The gift of gladness ages well. Be glad.

Today's Wisdom:

> I have only managed to live so long by carrying no hatreds.
>
> —Winston Churchill

Not Enough Hangers

Watch the path of your feet and
all your ways will be established.

—Proverbs 4:26

Does your closet look so full and cramped that nothing new can be added? Does your clothes pole look like it is going to break, where not one more shirt, blouse, or dress can fit into place?

If you have that "bunched in" problem at your house, join the club. Let's take a look at managing your stuff—the clutter that is taking over space you could be using for better purposes.

One rule that has helped us stay uncluttered at our house is best stated as, "One comes in and one goes out." After every purchase of clothing, we give away or place in our "garage-sale area" for a future garage sale the items being replaced by the new clothes. This practice also teaches children that balance is better than striving to accumulate items. Adults can learn the same lesson. This means that after every Christmas, you will need to really focus on giving away to other people. This practical idea becomes a wonderful holiday tradition.

Our church has an annual rummage sale, and all proceeds go to the support of missions. Each year we are amazed that other people want to purchase our junk. But they do, and our missionaries are blessed by this fund-raiser.

Have an annual garage sale or participate in a neighborhood sale. You can have a lot of fun and excitement, and you get to know your neighbors. Bob and I informed our loved ones that we do not want any more gifts that take up space or have to be dusted. At this stage in our lives, we prefer consumable items (like cruises, dinner gift certificates, hotel reservations for the weekend, etc.). We know parents who ask guests not to bring gifts for their small children's birthdays. When those toys start piling up and your child is overwhelmed with choices, it might be time to get creative with a child's clutter as well.

Remember, life is not based on your possessions. Keep your life simple. Remove the clutter. Do not go out and purchase more hangers to hang more stuff, but remember our rule: "One comes in and one goes out."

Prayer: *Father God, a simple lifestyle suits my trust in You. May I never get caught up in the need for things when I have so many richer pursuits before me: family, prayer, giving, obedience to You. Amen.*

Action: In each room get rid of items that you do not use.

Today's Wisdom:

All the beautiful sentiments in the world weigh less than a single lovely action.

—James Russell Lowell

Go to the ant, O sluggard,
observe her ways and be wise.

—PROVERBS 6:6

ave you ever taken the time to look at nature and consider the awesomeness of creation? I have, but not often enough. However, as a young girl living in Arizona, I remember one hot summer day when I had nothing to do (meaning I was bored). I became fascinated with hundreds of ants coming out of a raised anthill. To this day I am amazed at how energetic, strong, fast, and productive these little creatures are. For their size and weight, they are outstanding in what they can accomplish. We as grown humans should look at these creatures to see what the writer of Proverbs had in mind when he suggested to the sluggard (lazy person) to look at the ant—in other words to get off his lazy seat and get moving. A wise person is not lazy.

One of the most important skills you can ever learn in this life is how to form healthy habits—how to get into the habit of good habits. The experts tell us that it takes 21 days to form a new habit. Why habits? It is one more way to organize our time and our lives. And it is one more step toward giving priority to what God has called us to do with our lives. It starts with handling the routine jobs in our lives.

Start by thinking before you do routine jobs. The way that you perform basic tasks is usually the result of habit, not logic. Is there a better way? Why does a half-hour job often take twice as long as planned? It is probably because you estimated only the working time. Perhaps you forgot the time it takes to get everything set up. Make a habit of thinking before you start.

Also make it a habit to return everything to its proper place. One of my mottos is, "Do not put it down; put it away." Nothing wastes time like not knowing where you put something you need now. I remind women to store like things together. That way when you are working on a project you only have to go to one place to find what you are looking for. Do not be discouraged when forming new habits. Give yourself time. It took you a long time to form old habits, so do not expect overnight success. Start moving a pile of dirt, one shovelful at a time.

Prayer: *Father God, help me get rid of all those old habits that slow me down. Let me learn from the industriousness of the little ant. Amen.*

Action: In your mind think about an ant you have seen in your life. On a blank sheet of paper write down what you observed. Now imitate!

Today's Wisdom:

     We read books to find out who we are....It is an essential guide to our understanding of what we ourselves are and what we may become.

                         —Ursula K. LeGuin

You Must Toil for It

A little sleep, a little slumber,
a little folding of the hands to sleep.

—Proverbs 6:10

How often we hear, "I want it now. I do not want to work hard to get it, either. Please give me pleasure. I want the easy life." We have become a society of quick riches. We live in Southern California, and the state has given the Indian tribes permission to have gaming casinos on their land. These beautiful casinos are popping up everywhere. When you drive by them, you notice the parking lots are full. Masses of people are looking for the quick fix of becoming wealthy overnight.

Likewise, the California lottery payouts reach record-breaking amounts each time. We are a state full of people who want to get rich fast. Hard work, it seems, is no longer in fashion.

The "sluggard"—who could be male or female—is mentioned a number of times in the book of Proverbs. Her procrastination and lack of initiative are strongly condemned. Her foolishness is evident in her lack of preparation for the future; rather, she prefers to stay in bed (Proverbs 6:9-10). As she waits and does nothing, opportunities slip away. Without notice, poverty and need will overwhelm her.

God expects us to work. In fact, one of the very first work assignments God gave Adam and Eve was to take care of the garden of Eden. There are no easy jobs in life. Those who refuse to be industrious will eventually be rudely awakened from their daydreams, for desperate need and grinding poverty are sure to come (see Proverbs 24:30,34).

We, as parents, model to our children how we perceive work. If we respect hard work and proper stewardship of our money and things, our children will also reflect such values. However, if we model a get-rich-quick mentality, they will, too. Choose which model you will be.

Prayer:　　　*Father God, I certainly do not want to be known as a sluggard. Give me the proper respect for hard work and good stewardship of all the blessings You have given me. Amen.*

Action:　　　Be zealous in your work. Thank God for giving you the vision to prepare yourself for excellence.

Today's Wisdom:

The law of nature is that a certain quantity of work is necessary to produce a certain quality of good of any kind whatever. If you want knowledge, you must toil for it; if food, you must toil for it; and, if pleasure, you must toil for it.

—John Ruskin

Lord, help me over life's rough road
To share my brother's heavy load.
Since Christ bore mine for me.

—S. E. BURROW

Welcome Home

I have fellowship offerings at home;
today I fulfilled my vows.

—Proverbs 7:14 NIV

Have you ever considered your home to be a place where you can have "fellowship offerings"? Do those who reside in your home consider it a place where they feel welcome and can find peace, quiet, and solitude within its four walls? We have known friends who call home their "trauma center"—a place where dysfunction meets function, a place where hurting people can find healing.

My husband, Bob, and I have enjoyed nearly half a century of marriage, have raised two children, and have welcomed five delightful grandchildren from the ages of 10 to 21 years old. In my ministry I have had the opportunity to talk to thousands of women, and there are certain characteristics that seem to account for families in America with success, happiness, and strength.

These characteristics include an awareness that each member is appreciated and a voluntary desire to spend time together that is abundant in both quantity and quality. Create times of togetherness when your children are little so that it is natural for your family to sit and talk about or read from Scripture together. These traditions help build strong ties that hold fast when communication is at a low point. This leads to another important characteristic: good communication. Open communication is not just speaking, but also includes a lot of listening. During these times of open communication, be sure to be alert to verbal as well as nonverbal communication (body language). Often our body language transmits acceptance or rejection of ideas and thoughts. Let us also not forget conversation with a degree of religious orientation. Successful families also have a strong commitment to make the family and its members succeed. They talk about schooling and how to obtain added skills that will make each member successful. As a family, we prepare the members to have skills that give us the ability to deal with crisis in a positive manner.

If we could wake up each morning to the idea we were going to be a blessing to the members of our family no matter what, can you imagine the impact we would have? Go a step further, and think about how you can be a blessing to everyone you interact with this day. Wow! What a difference you can make. This is pretty simple but very profound!

Today make a vow to have a "fellowship offering" in your home. Let each member shout, "Home is so much fun! I am glad to be home."

Prayer: Father God, bless us with a strong family. May we seek Your Word and guidance as we build the foundation this family needs. May I be a blessing to my husband and to my children. Amen.

Action: Be a blessing to those around you today.

Today's Wisdom:
Success is neither fame, wealth, nor power, rather it is seeking, knowing, loving, and obeying God. If you seek, you will know; if you know, you will love; if you love, you will obey.

—Charles Malik

Seek and You Will Find

I love those who love me;
and those who diligently seek me will find me.

—Proverbs 8:17

*I*t seems that people today are looking for God in all the wrong places. The tabloids at the supermarket always have articles that tell the reader where to find God. Very seldom will you find a magazine that explains the "good news" that we as Christians understand and believe.

I came to know the Lord at age 16, and I have never really turned away from Him. I was raised in a Jewish home, and the only time I heard about Jesus was at Christmas. When I met my husband, he asked my mother if I could go to church with him and to my amazement she said yes. That was the beginning of my Christian journey. When I started to seek God, I was able to find Him through Jesus.

All of my writings have this theme of faithfulness woven through them, and many readers have told me they have been blessed by my writings. Faithfulness is not always easy! Each day I have to recommit to that youthful decision. Each day I struggle to maintain the discipline of Scripture reading and prayer, of taking myself off the throne and trusting God with my life. During my time of physical testing, the struggle was sometimes even harder because of sheer physical weakness and pain.

Sometimes, despite my best efforts, I have let the Lord down, but He has never let me down. That is really the secret of my faithfulness. I can be faithful to Him because He upholds me, strengthens me, forgives me—and promises that I will find Him if I seek Him. How can I not be faithful to an ever-faithful God?

Prayer: *Father God, I thank You for loving me. The best decision of my life has been when I accepted You as my Savior. Amen.*

Action: If you have not done so already, invite Jesus to be your Savior. It is a decision you will never regret. If you do know Jesus as your Savior, thank Him for His faithfulness to you.

Today's Wisdom:

The Rose

If you doubt there is a God, look deep into a rose;
See the velvet petals from the folded bud
    unclose;
Note the tine and texture and the lovely coloring;
Could blind Nature of itself evolve so fair a
    thing?
Feel the softness of the petal, breathe the fragrant
    scent;
Need you waste another thought on further
    argument?
Here is proof of a Creator: God made manifest;
In this little rose we see divinity expressed.

—Patience Strong

Seek Wisdom

From everlasting I [wisdom] was established, from the beginning, from the earliest times of the earth.

—PROVERBS 8:23

When I see that a business has been serving its clients since 1946, I subconsciously say, "That is a company I can trust." I know that it takes honesty, good products, and good service to stay in business that long. Only the best can survive in today's tough business climate.

But when I read that wisdom has been from the very beginning of creation, then I automatically say, "These proverbs regarding wisdom can be trusted. These thoughts have been around a long time, and they still endure the test of time."

Throughout Scripture we are urged to acquire knowledge. In these readings and instruction, we are told to have two goals in our life: wisdom (knowing and doing right) and common sense.

When we have wisdom, we are able to confront each situation with discernment and good and fair judgment, no matter what is required. We then become known as a wise person, because we have a history of good decisions. Wisdom goes beyond having knowledge (of course, knowledge does give us the opportunity to use the wisdom that God has given us through His Word).

When we humble ourselves before Christ, we let Him become our Source of wisdom. He will guide us, through the proper understanding of His Word, in making wise decisions and determining the proper course of action.

We have heard the old saying, "Just use common sense." The problem is that I find "common sense" to no longer be common. When you hear about the decisions some people make in their lives, you wonder if somewhere in life they missed the course in common sense. What seemed so common in the past is no longer common. Why do you think that to be true? I have a simple theory: I believe that few people are going to God's Word for information regarding decision making.

When a person has no benchmark (starting point) to make basic decisions in life, his or her decision making becomes random, erratic. This person turns to the world to find knowledge and becomes confused because of all the inconsistencies in the world's advice.

Stick with the tried and true, and you will discover that godly wisdom and common sense will make you a much-sought-after person for good advice.

Prayer: *Father God, give me wisdom and common sense. I want to be known as a person with good discernment. I want my decisions to be wise. Amen.*

Action: When you face a decision today, instead of looking to the world's wisdom, try to find direction in the Bible.

Today's Wisdom:

    Do you want to be counted wise, to build a reputation for wisdom? Here's what you do: Live well, live wisely, live humbly. It's the way you live, not the way you talk, that counts. Mean-spirited ambition isn't wisdom. Boasting that you are wise isn't wisdom. Twisting the truth to make yourselves sound wise isn't wisdom. It's the furthest thing from wisdom—it's animal cunning, devilish conniving. Whenever you are trying to look better than others or get the better of others, things fall apart and everyone ends up at the other's throats.

Real wisdom, God's wisdom, begins with a holy life and is characterized by getting along with others. It is gentle and reasonable, overflowing with mercy and blessings, not hot one day and cold the next, not two-faced. You can develop a healthy, robust community that lives right with God and enjoy its results *only* if you do the hard work of getting along with each other, treating each other with dignity and honor.

—James 3 THE MESSAGE

Create Table Art

When He established the heavens, I was there.

—PROVERBS 8:27

od certainly is a God of creativity. All we have to do is look around our environment and see all He has created: the universe, moon, stars, sun, mountains, plant life, and on and on. With His creativity He has given us the ability to create, too. Oh, do not tell me you are not creative. We *all* are to one extent or another. We just have to step out of our box and be encouraged to experiment with our artistic gifts. We can start using what we have around us—our prized possessions. We can create beauty by displaying the overflow from our cupboards on our tabletops.

No matter how much cupboard or closet space you have, it is still nice to have deliberately arranged objects on the top of tables, dressers, mantels, and windowsills. Decide which pieces you own that you would like to showcase.

To add interest to dresser tops (or to any flat surface in your home), create a "tablescape." It is simply an artfully arranged still life featuring items you love. For your husband's dresser, it could be a painted tray for pocket items or a group of photos in color-coordinated frames. Your dresser could display a round bowl of mixed flowers or a silk scarf draped over the mirror. In the guest room, leave one drawer partly open and drape a pair of long gloves or guest towels in the opening. Place a dish with peppermints or chocolate kisses on top of the dresser along with a small

Bible to encourage sweet, peaceful dreams. Add another nice touch with a few recent magazines and an up-to-date novel for good bedtime reading.

The benefit to "table art" is that the family is less likely to place other clutter on the surface. It actually keeps the room looking neater. So look around you. What creative tablescapes come to mind? Use your imagination, and some of the closet overflow and clutter will become miniature works of art. Keep it simple. Too much of anything can cause a different kind of clutter.

When you see how easy this project is, you will want to venture into other areas of creativity around your home.

Prayer: *Father God, fill my life with beauty. I will arrange my days to serve and follow You. I love all of Your creations. Amen.*

Action: Tie a ribbon on one chair at dinner. Whoever sits there gets the honor of saying the blessing.

Today's Wisdom:

    Love all God's creation, the whole and every grain of sand in it. Love every leaf, every ray of God's light.

               —Fyodor Dostoyevsky

□ □ □

Have a Teachable Spirit

Instruct a wise [woman] and [she]
will be wiser still; teach a righteous [woman]
and [she] will add to [her] learning.

—PROVERBS 9:9 NIV

*I*n sports we often hear that an athlete is a "coach's delight," which means this athlete is teachable, comes with an attitude to learn, and readily does what the coach suggests. In other words, this athlete is a great person to have on the team. This special person comes with a great attitude for teachability and is not a know-it-all.

Oh, how I pray for this important quality of character: a teachable heart. Since none of us is perfect, and life is filled with learning and growing day by day, having a teachable heart is the key to becoming all that God intended us to become.

A woman with a teachable heart is a priceless treasure. She has a heart that can give and forgive, protect and respect. Hers is a heart submitted to God above all. This is the woman that Proverbs says is "worth far more than rubies."

My daughter, Jenny, once gave me a beautiful, fragrant heart sachet as a gift. God was teaching me important lessons at the time about being a fragrance before Him and other people. That beautiful sachet always reminds me of the sweet fragrance of the Lord Jesus Himself. It also reminds me that I am called to be a woman after God's own heart.

I pray that His love might permeate your heart today in such a way that you will spread His fragrance to those around you. As surely as night follows day, a teachable heart produces the fragrance of His peace, His love, His joy!

Prayer: *Father God, I so want to be a coach's delight. I want to learn everything You have for me to learn. Give me the patience to learn as I go through life. Amen.*

Action: Learn one new thing today!

Today's Wisdom:

The world will never starve for want of wonders.
—Gilbert Keith Chesterton

☐ ☐ ☐

Add Years to Your Life

For by me your days will be multiplied,
and years of life will be added to you.

—PROVERBS 9:11

When I was a guest on *Focus on the Family*, Dr. James Dobson shared the above verse of Scripture with us. Since the name of our ministry is "More Hours in My Day," how appropriate this verse was. Truly God will give us more hours in our day if we will only apply His principles to our daily routine.

God always has daily promises for us in His Word, but we first have to read Scripture to find these golden nuggets. This promise is better than sliced bread, or better than a peanut-butter-and-jelly sandwich. The writer of Proverbs is saying, "I, wisdom, will make the hours of your day more profitable and the years of your life more fruitful."

We tell the ladies who come to our seminars and who read our books that they must have a plan for life. We cannot proceed successfully through life without a plan. A very important part of that plan is to start the day off in God's presence by reading Scripture, praying, and meditating on His promises and teachings. We must have a benchmark for all our decisions, and this benchmark starts with an understanding of who God is. All wisdom starts with this basic understanding.

If our lives are to reflect peace and tranquility, we must have that inner peace that only God can give. The world puts us on a fast-moving merry-go-round that goes faster and faster each day. At some point we must decide for ourselves how we will get out of this rat race. If not, we will be thrown off and get trampled by the crowd.

Prayer: *Father God, I accept Your promise that I will have a longer, fuller life by knowing You. Amen.*

Action:

- ✷ Start each day with God's Word.
- ✷ Be anxious for nothing. Give each day to the Lord.
- ✷ Be encouraging in whatever you do.
- ✷ Be in continual prayer.
- ✷ Give thanks in all things.

Today's Wisdom:

God wants us to know peace in every area of our lives—peace in our daily work, our business, our family, our soul. The key to letting peace enter in is to invite God into each of these areas daily.

—Elaine Creasman

Whom Will You Serve?

The woman of folly is boisterous,
she is naive and knows nothing.

—PROVERBS 9:13

What is a woman to do? On one hand she is instructed to be assertive, and on the other she is told to have a quiet and gentle spirit. The two do not mix. It is like mixing oil and water—impossible. If we listen to the world's advice, we will go the way of the power broker. Have you noticed in women's fashion the designers of women's apparel have told us by their design and full-page, high-gloss ads that black represents power? If a garment is black and adopts a masculine flair, then that is what successful wanna-be women will wear. We as women must ask ourselves if that is true. If not, what are the alternatives?

In Joshua 24:15 we read:

> If it is disagreeable in your sight to serve the LORD, choose for yourselves today whom you will serve: whether the gods which your fathers served which were beyond the River, or the gods of the Amorites in whose land you are living; but as for me and my house, we will serve the LORD.

That is the basic question for all of our lives: Are we going to serve the gods of the world, or are we going to serve the real God of our Christian faith? But for me, I have chosen to serve the Lord. I am not concerned about what the power brokers recommend. I am going to build my character upon the traits that God's Word presents to me.

I have chosen to be kind, loving, moderate, truthful, obedient, confident in who I am, prayerful, trustworthy, orderly, respectful, etc. This gives me all the confidence I need to live a fulfilled life in serving my husband, family, and God. I have chosen not to be a woman of folly who is boisterous. I pray that you will make a similar decision when you answer this basic question of life: "Whom will you serve?"

Prayer: *Father God, the best decision of my life has been to follow You as my Lord. You have given me such a joy and peace for life. I appreciate all You have done, are doing, and will do in the future. Amen.*

Action: Decide today whom you will serve.

Today's Wisdom:

     So be careful how you live, not as fools but as those who are wise. Make the most of every opportunity for doing good in these evil days. Don't act thoughtlessly, but try to understand what the Lord wants you to do.

         —Ephesians 5:15-17 NLT

□ □ □

Be Blessed at the Gates

*The memory of the righteous is blessed,
but the name of the wicked will rot.*

—PROVERBS 10:7

What a great formula for being remembered when
we are no longer on this earth: Be a righteous person and
you will be remembered.

On our communion table we read, "This do in remembrance of Me." Jesus passed on the legacy of breaking bread
and sipping a cup of wine in the upper room while He and
the disciples were celebrating the Passover. In order for them
(and us) to remember Jesus and this special occasion, He
left us the legacy of continuing to do this until He returns.
Because of Jesus' righteousness, He has been blessed and
remembered for more than 2000 years.

We, as women, can have the honor of being blessed by
those who know righteousness. "How?" you might ask. In
the passage on the virtuous woman in Proverbs 31:28 we
read, "Her children rise up and bless her; her husband also,
and he praises her." If you study this whole chapter, you
can see why she was blessed. Some of her righteous attri-
butes are:

- She was an excellent wife (verse 10).
- She had great worth (verse 10).
- Her husband trusted her (verse 11).

- She will not be a hindrance to his career (verse 11).

- She does her husband good (verse 12).

- She is a good worker, a good businesswoman, and a frugal shopper (verses 13-14,16).

- She is not lazy and provides food for her family (verse 15).

- She is healthy and strong (verse 17).

- She has self-confidence and works far into the night (verse 18).

- She is a skilled homemaker and craftsman (verse 19).

- She is generous to the poor and the needy (verse 20).

- She provides for her family before the cold weather sets in (verse 21).

- She has married a respected man in the city (verse 23).

- She is a tradesman in commerce (verse 24).

- She is optimistic and faces the future with a smile (verse 25).

- She is eloquent in speech. No harsh words come from her mouth (verse 26).

- She is energetic and always occupied (verse 27).

- She is noble of character (verse 29).

- She fears the Lord (verse 30).

- Her works bring her praise throughout the city (verse 31).

We hear the question asked, "What do women do all day?" We can see that womanhood done properly is a very demanding job. Weaklings need not apply. We can see by this passage that a righteous woman will be remembered long after she is gone.

Do you want to be this kind of woman? I know I do. It sounds so appealing. Is it easy? No, but it gives eternal rewards. No greater desire do I have, but to have my husband and children stand at the gates and call me blessed. Come on board. Let's try it together.

Prayer: *Father God, I want to leave a legacy of righteousness and blessing. I want to be remembered as a righteous woman who modeled the ways of being a godly woman. Thank You for giving me that desire. Amen.*

Action: Evaluate your life and see what needs to be done to be known as a righteous woman.

Today's Wisdom:

God asks no man whether he will accept life. That is not the choice. You must take it. The only choice is how.

—Henry Ward Beecher

Change Ugliness to Beauty

*Hatred stirs up strife, but love
covers all transgressions.*

—Proverbs 10:12

As we read the morning newspaper or view the evening news, we are saddened to read and hear of the tragic murder of children by restless, irresponsible people who decide that some young person should be killed. We seem to live in a hate-filled society that does not value another person's life. The visual media portrays life and death so casually. Special effects show people being blown up with no remorse on the part of the killer. It used to be only the bad guys died, but not anymore. Even the good guys are done away with. It is made to look so easy: boom-boom. As a society, we have become immune to violence and death. These are no longer a big deal.

However, if it is one of your own children in real life, it *is* a big deal. The media rarely show or tell about the people left behind when someone they love has been killed.

We often ask, "How do parents live through the murder of an innocent child?" Only through God's love can a heart of hate be changed to a heart of love.

A few years ago, Colombian rebels kidnapped Chet Bitterman, held him for 48 days, shot him, and left his body in a hijacked bus. Imagine how his parents and loved ones must have felt at the senseless death of this young American. More than a year later, as a demonstration of international goodwill, the churches and civic groups of Bitterman's native area, Lancaster County, Pennsylvania, gave an ambulance to the state of Meta in Colombia, where the young Wycliffe linguist was killed.

Bitterman's parents traveled to Colombia for the presentation of the ambulance. At the ceremony Chet's mother shared, "We are able to do this because God has taken the hatred from our hearts."

What an incredible act of love on the part of the parents! They took a most difficult situation and turned it into an act that presents the love of God. They knew that if they did not forgive the murderers, they would be victims for life, but if they could forgive, they would be victors for eternity.

Prayer: *Father God, I cannot imagine such love. What a wonderful example of loving your neighbor. May their lives be blessed forever. Amen.*

Action: Turn any hatred you have into an act of love.

Today's Wisdom:

Snow
that fell
so softly in the night
changed earth's soot to white
in glistening loveliness.

Forgiveness
like soft snow
gently covers the soil
and lo
ugliness is beauty.

—Lucille Gardner

Two Are Better Than One

When there are many words,
transgression is unavoidable, but [she]
who restrains [her] lips is wise.

—PROVERBS 10:19

We all have said something foolish and wished we had been quiet rather than opening our big mouth. How many times we have heard a politician, athlete, or movie star say something, and two days later there appears an apology for saying the wrong thing. It is human nature. The more we open our mouths, the greater opportunity we have to say the wrong thing.

Eleanor Roosevelt, the wife of one of our great presidents, stated,

> A mature person is one who does not think only in absolutes, who is able to be objective even when deeply stirred emotionally, who has learned that there is good and bad in all people and in all things, and who walks humbly and deals charitably with the circumstances of life. Knowing that in this world no one is all knowing and therefore all of us need both love and charity.

Today's Scripture talks about being more of a listener than a talker. Too many words can lead to putting our foot in our mouth. The more we speak, the greater our chance of being offensive. The wise woman will restrain her speech. God gave us one tongue to speak and two ears to hear. I guess He wanted us to hear twice as much as we speak. Listening seldom gets us into trouble, but our mouths certainly cause transgressions.

Prayer: *Father God, give me the courage to be a better listener. May I not be afraid to speak when appropriate. Give me wisdom to know when to speak. Amen.*

Action: Today concentrate on listening. Look the talker in the eye. Show that you are interested in what the other person is saying.

Today's Wisdom:

Let no unwholesome word proceed from your mouth, but only such a word as is good for edification according to the need of the moment, so that it will give grace to those who hear.

—Ephesians 4:29

Balance Your Scales

A false balance is an abomination to the LORD,
but a just weight is His delight.

—PROVERBS 11:1

If you are like I am, you hate to get on the scales in the bathroom. You step on and then peek at what the scale says. If it shows you have not gained weight, you are happy. But if you have gained a pound or two, your mouth turns down on the corners with a frown.

Scales and calculations play a big part in our country's economy. Everything seems to have a measurement, and we usually take for granted that the measurement is accurate. When we purchase meat, we expect a pound to be 16 ounces, a yard of fabric to be 36 inches, a gallon of milk to be four quarts, and a gallon of gas to be a gallon. I know I just take for granted that what I purchased is what I got. However, that has not always been true.

Before our government established an agency responsible for standards and weights, it was a very common practice for merchants to cheat on their scales. A consumer could not be sure that she was actually getting what was advertised or measured.

Today's proverb is a warning against such a practice. To cheat in business is something God frowns on, but He is delighted with an honest scale. That is not only true in business, but is a principle that is true in everyday life. We are to be women of character. Our yeses are to be yes and our nos are to be no.

When we hear that a business has been in operation for 40 or 50 years, we can be assured that the owners' balance scale has been accurate all these years. If it had not been, their customers would not have kept coming back.

Be a woman of character so that those around you will know that you can be trusted.

A story is told of a small country town where a young man entered a dry-goods store where his friend was the clerk. "Johnny," he said, winking slyly to the clerk, "you must give me good measure. Your master is not in." Johnny looked solemnly into the man's face and replied, "My Master is always in." Johnny's Master was the all-seeing God.

I am sure that Johnny had rehearsed that line long before his friend came into the store. We, too, need to be prepared in our response when someone wants us to cheat in life.

Prayer: *Father God, may my balance always be right. We have a lot of opportunities to lie in life. Let me remember that You, my Master, are an all-seeing God. Amen.*

Action: Check your scales to see if they are properly balanced. If not, adjust them.

Today's Wisdom:

I hope I shall always possess firmness and virtue enough to maintain what I consider the most enviable of all titles, the character of an "Honest Man."

—George Washington

Steer Your Ship

*Where there is no guidance the people fall, but in
abundance of counselors there is a victory.*

—Proverbs 11:14

The word *guidance* literally means "steering." I might ask, "Who is steering your ship in life?" As a parent, that is one of our most basic questions. Someone has to be making wise decisions regarding the family unit. It seems like in today's climate, the adults want to remain children. They dress like them, they talk like them, they like the same music and the same fashions, and on and on.

We are a country of adults who do not want to grow up. When we become adults, we are no longer children. We have to stand up and be responsible.

Paul, in his writing to the church at Corinth, expresses it very well: "When I was a child, I used to speak like a child, think like a child, reason like a child; when I became a man, I did away with childish things" (1 Corinthians 13:11). Paul is telling the Christians in the early church to stop being children of faith, to grow up in their faith and become mature.

Yes, it is much easier to remain as a child, but being an adult takes on new meaning. It is called responsibility. Our granddaughter at 16 wanted to be 21, but now that she is 21, she would like to be 16 again. Why? Because being an adult is not as much fun and requires more discipline.

One of the most difficult parts of being an adult is to take over the responsibility of steering the ship. A ship needs a master or it will be tossed to and fro and eventually crushed on the rocks and destroyed.

We live at the beach in Southern California, and there are thousands of boats in our harbor. The Coast Guard is always conducting classes on how to handle a vessel properly. There are also many parks and recreation programs all year round on various phases of properly handling a vessel. If a person wants to learn how to manage and steer a boat properly, there are plenty of opportunities to learn.

The same goes for managing a family. To us as parents (single or married), God has given the responsibility to seek proper counselors so we can gain information on how to run our family's ship. Our church offers parents all kinds of courses on how to steer their families so they will not be wrecked on the beach and destroyed. Seek out in your community various agencies which can offer you and your spouse skills in guiding your family.

One of the Barnes family mottos is, "If you fail to plan, you plan to fail." No one wants to be a failure, so seek a qualified counselor who can help you steer your family.

Prayer: *Father God, help me steer my family. At times I feel lost at sea, but a few more skills might help me prevent a shipwreck. I look to You as my chief Counselor. Amen.*

Action: Develop with your mate a plan for giving guidance to your family.

Today's Wisdom:

I came about like a well-handled ship. There stood at the wheel that...steersman whom we call God.

—Robert Louis Stevenson

□ □ □

You Cannot Outgive God

One [woman] gives freely, yet gains even more;
another withholds unduly, but comes to poverty.
A generous [woman] will prosper; [she] who
refreshes others will [herself] be refreshed.

—PROVERBS 11:24-25 NIV

I have found this to be a basic principle in life:
Giving pays tremendous dividends. Most of our riches are
in friends, support groups, and those who give encouragement. As we have refreshed other people, the Lord has
refreshed us through these gifts of special people.

One of my favorite mottos has been, "You cannot outgive God." Mark tells us in his Gospel that if we give up
worldly possessions for Christ, we shall receive a hundred
times in the present age these things: homes, brothers, sisters, mothers, children, and land (Mark 10:29-30). Wow!
What a return of blessings for those who serve God.
Scripture is full of stories of God blessing those who are
faithful. It starts out small, but ends up bigger; that is, if we
are faithful first to the little things of life. It matters not how
much your wealth is, but what you do with the portion He
has given you. By stepping out in faith—that of a mustard
seed—we are able to move mountains.

Our heavenly Father wants to give us His bountiful harvest. First we prepare the soil, plant the seed, fertilize, hoe
the weeds, water when needed, and then bring in the harvest. Nature requires that we sow before we are able to
receive the harvest. If we have been generous in giving,

prayer, and preparation, we will receive in return an abundance at harvesttime.

Prayer: Father God, the principle of giving has been the best thing You have shared with me. My life is so much richer because of what You have taught me. Thank You! Amen.

Action: Find a unique way to give yourself away today.

Today's Wisdom:

Giving is a joy if we do it in the right spirit. It all depends on whether we think of it as, "What can I spare?" or as "What can I share?"
—Esther York Burkholder

I will fling open wide a door of hope,
And I will give you back
Years that the locusts have devoured;
No good thing shall you lack.

—NANCY HANSEN

No Greater Love

A wife of noble character is her husband's crown,
but a disgraceful wife is like decay in his bones.

—PROVERBS 12:4 NIV

*M*ajor Sullivan Ballou wrote this letter to his devoted wife, Sarah, a week before Manassas, the first battle of Bull Run. Sarah must have been a wife of noble character who truly was a crown to her soldier husband.

July 14, 1861
Camp Clerk, Washington, D.C.

My very dear Sarah,
 The indications are very strong that we shall move in a few days—perhaps tomorrow. Lest I should not be able to write again, I feel impelled to write a few lines that may fall under your eye when I shall be no more....
 I have no misgivings about, or lack of confidence in, the cause in which I am engaged, and my courage does not halt or falter. I know how strongly American Civilization now leans on the triumph of the Government, and how great a debt we owe to those who went before us through the blood and sufferings of the Revolution. And I am willing—perfectly willing—to lay down all my joys in this life, to help maintain this Government, and to pay that debt.
 Sarah, my love for you is deathless; it seems to bind me with mighty cables that nothing but Omnipotence could break; and yet my love of Country comes over me

like a strong wind and bears me unresistibly on with all these chains to the battlefield.

The memories of the blissful moments I have spent with you come creeping over me, and I feel most gratified to God and to you that I have enjoyed them so long. And hard it is for me to give them up and burn to ashes the hopes of future years, when, God willing we might still have lived and loved together, and seen our sons grow up to honorable manhood, around us. I have, I know, but few and small claims upon Divine Providence, but something whispers to me—perhaps it is the wafted prayer of my little Edgar, that I shall return to my loved ones unharmed. If I do not, my dear Sarah, never forget how much I love you, and when my last breath escapes me on the battlefield, it will whisper your name. Forgive my many faults, and the many pains I have caused you. How thoughtless and foolish I have often times been! How gladly would I wash out with my tears every little spot upon your happiness....

But, O Sarah! if the dead can come back to this earth and flit unseen around those they loved, I shall always be near you; in the gladdest days and in the darkest nights...*always, always,* and if there be a soft breeze upon your cheek, it shall be my breath, as the cool air fans your throbbing temple, it shall be my spirit passing by. Sarah, do not mourn me dead; think I am gone and wait for thee, for we shall meet again.[6]

Sullivan Ballou was killed at the first battle of Bull Run, leaving his wife these few beautiful lines of love. She undoubtedly thought of her beloved husband whenever a soft breeze touched her cheek. Her husband had been both strong and sensitive, both tough and tender. As his letter reflects, he faced death with courage, standing strong in his convictions and unwavering in his commitment to his country, his wife, and his God. And I would guess that some of his courage resulted from a wife who believed in him, encouraged him, and made him her hero.

Supporting your man will indeed encourage him to be the man—and husband and father—that God wants him to be. Like Sullivan Ballou, who was both tough and tender, your husband can come to know the strength of his masculinity. He can know the balance between strong and sensitive that God intended when He made man. I am sure God looked down upon Major Ballou and said, "It was good." You can help your man earn those same words of praise, and he will praise you at the gates.

May we all strive to be a wife of noble character and our husband's crown.[7]

Prayer: *Father God, I desire to be a woman of character. I want to find pleasure in Your sight, and I want to be a crown to my husband. Please bring into my life those women who will show me how to develop Christian character. May my husband be receptive to my changes. I so want him to know that I love him very much. I never want to be a disgrace to him. Amen.*

Action: Set out today to be a woman of noble character.

Today's Wisdom:

Do not pray for easy lives, pray to be stronger men [and women]. Do not pray for tasks equal to your powers; pray for powers equal to your tasks. Then the doing of your work shall be no miracle, but you shall be a miracle. Every day you shall wonder at yourself, at the richness of life which has come to you by the grace of God.

—Phillips Brooks

□ □ □

Never Too Young

*A [woman] will be satisfied with good
by the fruit of [her] words, and the deeds of
a [woman's] hands will return to [her].*

—Proverbs 12:14

As a mom and now a grandmother, I am happy to pass along some tips for teaching children responsibility. Believe me, these ideas will also make your life easier. Do not be afraid to begin teaching even your littlest child how to help out.

Make a place mat out of butcher paper and draw the shapes of the fork, plate, spoon, and knife. Your child gets to put each item in its proper place. Give him or her a pillowcase to pick up toys, trash, and newspapers around the house and even in the yard. Help your child to dress independently. If you buy coordinates, any top will go with any bottom. In the closet you can hang up one pair of pants followed by the shirt to match. That way they not only know what matches what, but they can help you put the clothes away after you do the laundry. Young boys and girls can be taught to iron flat items like napkins, pillowcases, and linens. Just give them a lesson on how to handle a hot iron.

When your children are ready to put away toys, have boxes, bins, or low shelves for them to use. If children are to be organized, they must have proper tools. And do not forget to let them do it their way—arranged by them and not by you. While this can be a tough one, it really does help children develop a system that makes sense to them. If they create the method, they will remember it and be more likely to follow it. In other words, make chores fun!

I found that having the children help sort the laundry was a big help to me, and it also taught them some laundry skills. I would take three large bags, bins, or containers. One would be white, one dark, and one mixed colors. The children could sort their dirty clothes in one of the three containers. White items would go into the white container, dark clothes would go into the dark container, and the mixed-color clothing would go into the mixed-color container. Just this amount of help saved me a lot of time doing laundry since everything was presorted!

Prayer: *Father God, I want to pass along the goodness of hard work. Help me to have a servant's heart as I teach my children responsibilities. Amen.*

Action: Walk your children through some basic tasks. Continue this until they can do them with confidence.

Today's Wisdom:

It is not what you expect, but what you inspect.

☐ ☐ ☐

She May Be Right

*The way of a fool is right in [her] own eyes, but a
wise [woman] is [she] who listens to counsel.*

—PROVERBS 12:15

I do not know about you, but I hate to be criticized. However, as a writer and speaker, I have occasionally had the opportunity to receive harsh words from my listeners or my readers (fortunately, not too many over the 20-plus years).

However, one critical word seems to resound in my spirit more than 20 compliments. At first my reaction was to fight back and defend myself. But then I remembered that early in my ministry I had read about a pastor speaking on this subject. He, too, had received harsh words from people in his congregation. This is what he said: "Every piece of criticism can be helpful. God may be in it, and if He is, I need to hear what He is saying. The critic might be right."

I heeded this advice and began to look at the critic in a different light. What truth might there be in the harsh remarks? Obviously the critic felt very strongly about the subject, or the person would not have taken the time to share the thoughts with me.

There are several biblical principles that I use when I am taken to task for something I have said or written:

> ❧ *Do not respond in anger.* It will only increase the
> tension between you (Proverbs 15:1).

ༀ *This is an opportunity for me to model Christlike behavior.* After all, we are to be doers of God's Word (Philippians 2:1-4).

ༀ *The critic may be right.* I may need to change. A wise person is to seek counsel (Proverbs 9:8-9).

David Egner states, "Treat a critic as a friend, and you both win." This really takes a lot of Christian maturity. Our first reaction is usually not that positive, but learning to respond to criticism with wisdom is an important part of living the Christian life.

Prayer: Father God, continue to give me wise counsel in relating to my critics. I certainly need Your support in this area. Let Your love overflow in my life. Amen.

Action: See what truth God is teaching you through the eyes of your critic.

Today's Wisdom:

Most of us associate being criticized with being punished or told we're unwanted, and often it bears this implication, especially when parents criticize their children. Only by forcing ourselves to listen to criticism can we teach ourselves that it is sometimes well intended, and that we won't fall to pieces no matter what other people say about us.

—George Weinberg

☐ ☐ ☐

Use Wisdom When Speaking

The tongue of the wise brings healing.

—PROVERBS 12:18

As a young girl I was so shy. In fact, those close to me would ask, "Has the cat got your tongue?" It was not until I met my future husband, Bob, that I had enough confidence to talk openly. It has been estimated that a woman speaks about 30,000 words in a day, and men speak about half that amount. The important question is, "How do our words affect people around us?"

Solomon wrote, "The tongue of the wise brings healing" (Proverbs 12:18). The tongue of the wise affirms and encourages other people. The word of emphasis is not *tongue* but *wise*. The tongue is not in control, but the person behind it is.

A Greek philosopher asked his servant to cook the best dish possible. The servant, who was very wise, prepared a dish of tongue, saying, "It is the best of all dishes, for it reminds us that we may use the tongue to bless and express happiness, dispel sorrow, remove despair, and spread cheer."

Later the servant was asked to cook the worst dish possible. Again he prepared a dish of tongue, saying, "It is the worst dish, for it reminds us that we may use the tongue to curse and break hearts, destroy reputations, create strife, and set families and nations at war."

The servant's point was that our tongue can be the best or it can be the worst. We as individuals will determine the quality of our words. We decide the power of our words. Will they be words of encouragement, or words that tear down?

Prayer: *Father God, let me use wisdom when I speak. Let me be one who is an edifier not a destroyer. I so want my words to build up, not tear down. Amen.*

Action: Mind your speech today.

Today's Wisdom:

You will never be an inwardly religious and devout man [or woman] unless you pass over in silence the shortcomings of your fellow men, and diligently examine your own weaknesses.

—Thomas à Kempis

☐ ☐ ☐

Swear to Tell the Truth

Lying lips are an abomination to the LORD, but those who deal faithfully are His delight.

—PROVERBS 12:22

Court scenes are exciting to me. I love the formality of the swearing in of a witness as he puts his left hand on the Bible, raises his right hand, and swears "to tell the truth, so help me God."

I sometimes wonder if people know the truth anymore. Even when a person is guilty without a doubt, he enters a plea of "not guilty." I would be shocked if a murderer would stand before the judge and say, "I'm guilty as charged."

I recently received a flier from my car-insurance carrier that listed some of the excuses given by policyholders of why an accident happened. The following are just a few that people gave to the insurance carrier:

- "An invisible car came out of nowhere, struck my car and vanished."

- "I had been driving my car for 40 years when I fell asleep at the wheel and had the accident."

- "I pulled away from the side of the road, glanced at my mother-in-law, and headed over the embankment."

- "The pedestrian had no idea which direction to go, so I ran over him."

❧ "The telephone pole was approaching fast. I attempted to swerve out of its path, when it struck my front end."

❧ "The guy was all over the road. I had to swerve a number of times before I hit him."

These are humorous stories as we read them, but they point out how we try to shade the facts, especially when we are trying to convince someone that it was not our fault. I am sure the insurance agent would love to hear, "Sorry, but it was my fault. I caused the accident."

Today's verse challenges us to speak the truth—and nothing but the truth.

Prayer: *Father God, seal my lips from saying anything other than the truth. Let me be brave when I am asked the particulars of a situation. I trust in Your justice for my life. Amen.*

Action: If you have an opportunity today, do not hedge to protect yourself, but tell the truth.

Today's Wisdom:

The New Testament does not say, "You shall know the rules, and by them you shall be bound," but, "You shall know the truth, and the truth shall make you free."

—John Baille

Do Not Be Under the Circumstances

Anxiety in a [woman's] heart weighs it down,
but a good word makes it glad.

—PROVERBS 12:25

Today we are a country of anxious people. Even before we get out of bed in the morning, our minds race through our schedule for the hectic day that lies ahead. I recently watched a TV program where a father was racing to work and forgot he had his two-year-old son in the backseat. His thoughts were so much on his morning sales meeting that he forgot to drop the boy off at the baby sitter, drove right past the sitter's home, and drove directly to work, parked his car as usual, and went into work to finalize his sales presentation. Two hours later a fellow employee noted that the young boy was in a car seat in the backseat of this man's car. It was a very hot day, and all the windows were rolled up in the car. The man went inside to tell the unsuspecting father of his son's situation. You guessed it! The boy had died of heat exhaustion. What a price to pay for anxiety!

Anxiety in our hearts does weigh us down. We all know about that. Think of the times that our joy has been robbed because of this sin. I always say that 85 percent of the things we worry about never happen. So stop worrying. What is a good word that can make a worrier glad? A word from the Lord. His words are always perfectly suited to our situation: a word of love, forgiveness, hope, joy. When anxiety and worry weigh us down, we need to tell the Lord how we feel and tell Him what is distressing us, then bend an ear heavenward and listen to His reply.

On occasion we get a pebble in our shoe that feels like it is a boulder. As we take off our shoe and dump out the small rock, we are amazed that such a small element caused us so much pain. At one time or another we all have pebbles in our shoe. Often they feel like huge problems until we examine them and break them into small elements. Who or what in your life is causing this worry and anxiety? Jesus says, "Trust Me. I am able to help you get through any of life's burdens." Lay your anxieties at the foot of the cross, and do not take them back. You will be amazed that 85 percent of your worries never have to be dealt with, and the other 15 percent can be examined and handled in small segments. Do not allow a small pebble to become a boulder in your life.

Prayer: Father God, keep me from making pebbles into boulders. You are my Source of strength and encouragement. Give me the patience to deal with each burden in a Christian fashion. Amen.

Action: Turn your burdens over to God, and search Scripture to find peace in your situation.

Today's Wisdom:
A great many people are trying to make peace, but that has already been done. God has not left it for us to do; all we have to do is to enter into it.
—Dwight L. Moody

□ □ □

Praying God's Will

A wise son [or daughter] accepts [their] father's discipline, but a scoffer does not listen to rebuke.

—PROVERBS 13:1

*J*esus used children as an illustration of the faith, trust, loyalty, and submission to God which are required in order to become part of His kingdom. The sharing of the gospel with children must be a priority at home and at church. All believers have the assignment to model a godly life before the children around them and to love these little ones and tell them about the Lord.

The gospel message is to be given to all, and a response is required by all who are old enough to know the difference between right and wrong (Matthew 28:19-20). Children are very capable of responding to God in praise, worship, prayer, and thanksgiving.

In Matthew 18:6 He states, "Whoever causes one of these little ones who believe in Me to stumble, it would be better for him to have a heavy millstone hung around his neck, and to be drowned in the depth of the sea."

That is a very serious statement of consequences, and therefore I want to do everything within my power to take it seriously. We are to be teachers and edifiers with proper instruction for our children. In my book *Fill My Cup, Lord*, I talk about a cup of prayer (as found in Colossians 1:9-14). I want parents to learn how to pray for their children. These little ones (or big ones—they still remain your children even though they are grown adults) need a hedge of prayer daily. A series of books that I find most helpful in praying the Scriptures for my children and grandchildren is written by Lee Roberts (Thomas Nelson Publishers): *Praying God's Will for My Son* and *Praying God's Will for My Daughter*.

These resources quote Scripture and let you insert the children's specific names so you can personalize your prayers. I have literally worn out my one book while praying for my daughter these past 2½ years. One of the side effects is that I see changes taking place in my own life. Oh, the Lord is certainly working in Jenny's life because of all my prayers, but He is truly performing a miracle in my own life as well.

My friend Donna states, "Let's face it, without prayer anything else you do to influence your children for Jesus is feeble at best." In her book *The Stay-at-Home Mom* she lists ten ways in which a mother can pray for her children.

1. Pray that your children will fear the Lord and serve Him (Deuteronomy 6:13).

2. Pray that your children will know Christ as Savior early in life (Psalm 63:1).

3. Pray that your children will be caught when they're guilty (Psalm 119:71).

4. Pray that your children will desire the right kind of friends and be protected from the wrong kind (Proverbs 1:10,15).

5. Pray that your children will be kept from the wrong mate and saved for the right one (2 Corinthians 6:14).

6. Pray that your children and their prospective mates will be kept pure until marriage (1 Corinthians 6:18-20).

7. Pray that your children will be teachable and able to take correction (Proverbs 13:1).

8. Pray that your children will learn to submit totally to God and actively resist Satan in all circumstances: "Submit therefore to God" (James 4:7).

9. Pray that your children will be hedged in so they cannot find their way to wrong people or wrong places, and that wrong people cannot find their way to your children (Hosea 2:6-7).

10. Pray that your children will honor their parents so all will go well with them.[8]

The only assurance I have of access to my children's hearts is through prayer and the power of the Holy Spirit. Your children will give you reasons to pray. If you have never been on your knees in prayer for your children, you will be when they become teenagers. Up goes your time in prayer.

Prayer: *Father God, I have been challenged again today to be in earnest prayer for my children. As I survey the world and its changing attitudes toward children, I want to be a shining beacon supporting them in every way possible. You have inspired me to care for all of their other needs in life. Now You have placed on my heart a burden to pray and instruct them in the ways of the Lord. Amen.*

Action: Make a prayer notebook page for each of your children. Take a recent photo of each one and paste it at the top of the first page for each. Have them lay their outstretched hand on the top of the first page. Trace around their fingers so you will have the outline of their hand etched on the first page. In the middle of the handprint, draw a small heart. Each time you pray for that child, place your hand upon the handprint, so your heart beats with your child's heartbeat.

Use these pages to write down specific prayer requests for each child, date the entry, and save room for listing the date when God answers that specific prayer request. Show the pages to your children so that they know you are a praying mom.

Today's Wisdom:

The Reverend Moses Browne had 12 children. When someone remarked to him, "Sir, you have just as many children as Jacob," he replied, "Yes, and I have Jacob's God to provide for them."

*For we do not have a high priest who cannot
sympathize with our weaknesses,
but One who has been tempted
in all things as we are,
yet without sin.*

—HEBREWS 4:15

□ □ □

Abundantly Satisfied

The soul of the sluggard craves and gets nothing,
but the soul of the diligent is made fat.

—Proverbs 13:4

*T*he word *fat* in this verse does not mean "obese" as in our present condition in America, but it refers to being "abundantly satisfied." Satisfaction is a wonderful virtue. Many years ago Bob's manufacturing company took about 150 prize-winning distributors on a week's vacation in Jamaica. While there, we observed the contrast between our group of Americans and the Jamaican people.

Our people were complaining that the humidity was so bad, it was so hot, sunburns were gotten too easily, the food was too spicy, and so on. However, the Jamaican ladies who cleaned our wonderful accommodations were smiling, humming, and singing praises to our Lord. One group knew how to be satisfied, and the others did not. One of our family sayings is, "If you are not satisfied with what you have, you'll never be satisfied with what you want." In Philippians 4:11, Paul states, "I have learned to be content in whatever circumstance I am." That is being abundantly satisfied.

One way we can be "abundantly satisfied" is to be a planner of our activities. Do not just run around putting out fires. Failing to plan the day is one of the top time-wasters. It goes right along with putting things off or trying to do everything yourself. You must learn to delegate. When Plan A is not working, you must move on to Plan B.

It is time to get back to the basics. Start today to make it a priority to plan your day, before the day plans you. Group your errands and tasks together—telephone calls, cooking, letter-writing, bill-paying, shopping—and schedule blocks of time to get each group done.

Here is a big one to work on: Promise less, deliver more. Remember, if you cannot manage your time, you will not be able to manage any other part of your life. As someone has well said, "Time is a daily treasure that attracts many robbers." There are many things that will steal your time and rob you of the focus you need to follow the Lord in the things He has called you to do. Be aware; you are protecting a valuable treasure.

Today set aside at least an hour of personal time to replenish your body, your mind, and your soul. Let the Lord give you discipline to break bad habits of neglect and develop new ones of healthy concern and responsibility. You can do it and, if you do, God promises that you will be abundantly satisfied.

Prayer: *Father God, teach me to discipline my mind. I am so distracted by all the sights and sounds of this age. I want to set my heart on You today. I delight to sing Your praises. Amen.*

Action: Write in your journal two bad habits you want to break. Under each listing jot down what you will do to break the habits. To the right of each listing, write down the date by which you want to accomplish the task. Leave room to also write the date when the habit was broken.

Today's Wisdom:

Life is not made up of great sacrifices and duties,
But of little things; in which smiles
And kindness and small obligations,
Given habitually, are what win and
Preserve the heart and secure comfort.

—Humphry Davy

What a friend we have in Jesus,
All our sins and griefs to bear!
What a privilege to carry
Ev'rything to God in prayer.

—JOSEPH SCRIVEN

Financial Freedom

*Wealth obtained by fraud dwindles, but the one
who gathers by labor increases it.*

—Proverbs 13:11

In recent years we have witnessed many, many individuals—both men and women—who have tried to gather wealth by fraud. This has happened not only in business, but also in sports, politics, religious organizations, the entertainment world, etc. The list goes on and on of individuals trying to gather wealth beyond what the ethics of their profession allows. There are certain rules, both written and unwritten, by which we are expected to play. When we break these rules, it is called fraud. Many of these people face not only embarrassment, but also defrocking from their profession, large fines, and even prison terms in some cases. God says we are not to gather wealth by fraud.

In many of our books, we try to lay out some basic financial principles that will lead an individual to financial freedom. We emphasize three basic principles:

- God owns everything; He merely loans things to us as we show Him our ability to be good stewards of what He owns.

- Money is a resource used to accomplish other goals and obligations you have for your life purpose. Money is never an end by itself.

෴ Have less expenditures than you do income, and you will have extra money to save, invest, and share.

There is a great amount of freedom when we know and believe that God owns everything. It takes away the idea that "I did it all by myself" and "I am a self-made person." One of our short- and long-term goals is to cover the financial aspects of our life. Do not rely on luck to give you financial security. You must have a plan, then work your plan.

The average person who understands these three concepts will over time become financially independent. We define *success* as "a progressive realization of worthwhile goals." You have to be willing to postpone or delay immediate gratification. This is contrary to present-day thinking. The world says, "Get it now. Why wait?" The Lord says, "Slow down. In time I will give you the desires of your heart."

Prayer: *Father God, please help me implement these principles so I can be a better steward of Your resources. Give me the patience to take a long-term view of what wealth and success are. Amen.*

Action: Establish a short- and long-term goal to make you and your family financially independent. Learn ways to make money grow little by little.

Today's Wisdom:

Whoever sows sparingly will also reap sparingly, and whoever sows generously will also reap generously. Each man should give what he has decided in his heart to give, not reluctantly or under compulsion, for God loves a cheerful giver.

—2 Corinthians 9:6-7 NIV

Living Your Dream

Desire realized is sweet to the soul.

—PROVERBS 13:19

I would be happy if only I had a new home, a better car, more money, a better job. Have these thoughts crossed your mind before? All of us have played the "if only" game.

Did you know that God has already given you your dream home? It is the one you are in. That is true. Even if you are just starting out, the place you have can be a comfortable—and even beautiful—home!

Get yourself some spray paint and get started. Spray white paint on an old wrought-iron lawn table, and you have a sturdy dining table. Sew some eyelet-lace curtains for your windows. Bob and I started out in our first apartment with a canvas chair, a wooden apple box for a lamp table, and an old trunk for a coffee table. I found that if I looked at everyday items with a little different perspective, I found clever uses for them. Ornate family or flea-market silverware arranged in a bright-blue terra-cotta pot makes a functional and never-fading arrangement for the table or kitchen countertop. Draping scarves over the arms of worn chairs gives them new life and personality. Even a few bright, decorative pillows make a sofa come alive. Everywhere you turn, ideas are waiting to be born. Be alert to life and observe what other people are doing. While reading your favorite ladies' magazine, tear out a photo of a design feature you like. Add it to a folder for future reference.

As you dream, as you plan, build, and decorate, you will gradually create your dream home. And remember, your present home is your dream home. The only rules to follow are your rules. If a particular color makes you smile, paint a chair, a room, or even a wooden crate in this happy hue. Best of all, as you explore what you like, you are creating a place you can share with family and friends, a place where you can raise your children in the love and admonition of the Lord. Sounds pretty good, doesn't it?

Do not be afraid to experiment with design and color. Let this concept even flow to the exterior of the home. After all, the first impression of your dream home is the design and flow of the yard (front and back). Whoever said that being a homemaker was not challenging enough never took time to stand back and see all the opportunities to be creative.

Prayer: *Father God, I dream of a loving, beautiful home that nurtures myself and my family. May You bless the home I am creating today. Amen.*

Action: When the children head off to school, light a candle to calmly prepare you for the rest of the day.

Today's Wisdom:

What is the good of a home if you are never in it?

—George Grossmith

Out of Abundance

A good man leaves an inheritance
for his children's children.

—PROVERBS 13:22 NIV

any grandparents have said to me, "I've raised my children. Now let them raise their children. My husband and I are sailing into the good old golden years." For some reason, our graying population wants to take the easy way out. "I have met my obligation. Now it is time to travel and have fun," is a common belief. Yes, there is truth in some of that, but Scripture gives us another challenge.

Not too many years ago, we were challenged to have a trust and a living will drawn up by our attorney, who specializes in this area of the law. We knew that because of the way tax laws are written, if something would happen to us, our estate would be locked up in a mass of tax laws and regulations.

As we were deciding how our estate would be divided, this particular verse challenged us to leave part of our worldly possessions to our five grandchildren. Not only were they listed as beneficiaries, but we set up an account (California Gift to Minors) with our stockbroker. Every birthday and at Christmas we make a contribution to these accounts. We figure that toys and clothes will have little value when they get to 18 years old, but a stock account will grow with time.

In the process, our grandchildren have learned about mutual and equity funds. They take a keen interest in learning how their particular funds are doing. What a delight for us to see them take an interest in their financial matters.

Prayer: *Father God, through Your abundance to us we have been challenged to help provide for our children's children. Thank You for that little nudge. Amen.*

Action: Make an appointment with your stockbroker and attorney to investigate the options your state offers for living trusts and other investment opportunities.

Today's Wisdom:

A generous man will prosper; he who refreshes others will himself be refreshed.

—Proverbs 11:25 NIV

Behold, I stand at the door and knock;
if anyone hears My voice and opens the door,
I will come in to him and will dine with him,
and he with Me.

—REVELATION 3:20

More Than a Flier of Kites

*The wise woman builds her house, but the foolish
tears it down with her own hands.*

—PROVERBS 14:1

en Franklin was one of our great founding
fathers. His writings and speeches exhibit true wisdom.
More than 200 years after he wrote *Poor Richard's Almanac*,
it is still read and respected for having so much wisdom
written within its pages. Ben Franklin used the *Almanac* as
a way of teaching the early colonists how to be frugal. It
was a painless way to impart some basic principles in order
for the colonists to survive living off the land's natural
resources.

Even though times have changed from rural to urban
life for most of us, Franklin's philosophy and principles of
living are still very useful. Here are a few of his guiding principles:

- A good example is the best sermon.

- A long life may not be good enough, but a good
  life is long enough.

- Great beauty, great strength, and great riches are
  really and truly of no great use; a right heart
  exceeds all.

- Content makes poor men rich; discontent makes
  rich men poor.

⌐ Who is rich? He that rejoices in his portion.

⌐ Search others for their virtues; thyself for vices.

⌐ The doors of wisdom are never shut.

These are all biblical principles that can and should be taught to our children. The book of Proverbs is filled with these principles of wisdom.

Prayer: *Father God, You are awesome. You are the Giver of all wisdom: Our most acceptable service that we can render to You is doing good to Your other children. Amen.*

Action: Tonight read aloud a few of Ben Franklin's guiding principles to your family and ask them to make up some of their own wise sayings about life. Print them on a sheet of paper and post it on your refrigerator for future reading.

Today's Wisdom:

Let not the wise man glory in his wisdom, neither let the mighty man glory in his might, let not the rich man glory in his riches; but let him that glorieth glory in this, that he understandeth and knoweth me, that I am the LORD which exercise lovingkindness, judgment, and righteousness, in the earth: for in these things I delight, saith the LORD.

—Jeremiah 9:23-24 KJV

Children Love Boundaries

He who withholds his rod hates his son, but he who
loves him disciplines him diligently.

—PROVERBS 13:24

o we ever ask the question, "What's happening
to our children?" Recently I read where the teenage suicide
rate is up. The statistics are quite alarming for the last few
decades. The reasons given for such an increase included:

- ❧ *Drugs and alcohol*—These were around in my
  youth, but I never recall a teenager dying from
  suicide because of drugs and alcohol. Maybe an
  occasional adult did, but never a teenager.

- ❧ *Economic insecurity*—I was a post-Depression
  child. My parents struggled to put food on the
  table, pay the rent, buy necessities for the family.
  But there were no teenage suicides because of
  someone's parents' economic status.

- ❧ *Changing values*—Values have always changed.
  We live in an age of flux. My parents disap-
  proved of my hair, clothes, and music. I thought
  the same about our children's values. So it will
  be for future generations. But there were no
  teenage suicides because of this.

- ❧ *Stress and alienation*—Those factors have
  always been with us. But back then, we had

people around us who cared—adults who were not afraid to be authority figures. However, today we live in an even faster-paced society, which no doubt adds to the stress level.

Maybe our question should be, "What's happening to our *adults?*" Parents, teachers, pastors, law enforcement officers, judges, and adults at large have a responsibility toward our younger generations. If we all abdicate at once, where is a child to turn for guidance?

There is certain validity in "Spare the rod, spoil the child." This is a very controversial subject, particularly in today's politically correct climate. However, I believe that children need the assurances of a disciplined life. It must be done in love and by parents who do not discipline out of anger. Children need discipline which is properly enforced by a loving parent.

Bob and I often said that the air was cleared after a session of discipline. It makes me think of Hebrews 12:11 which reads, "No discipline is enjoyable while it is happening—it is painful! But afterwards there will be a quiet harvest of right living for those who are trained in this way" (NLT).

Yes, children love boundaries. Boundaries give them a sense of being loved. With discipline, children are made to feel secure. Giving children proper guidance is one of the most difficult responsibilities that a parent has. In the Hebrew language, *parent* means "teacher." We are called to be a teacher—not a playmate, not a coequal, but a teacher. Remember, you are the adult and they are the children.

Prayer: *Father God, give me the courage to give proper discipline to my children. Society makes me confused about what is proper in this area, but Your Word has challenged me to be strict and firm, showing my love while disciplining. Amen.*

Action: Be a teacher to your children today—not a best buddy.

Today's Wisdom:

Discipline is demanded of the athlete to win a game. Discipline is required for the captain running his ship. Discipline is needed for the pianist to practice for the concert. Only in the matter of personal conduct is the need for discipline questioned. But if parents believe standards are necessary, then discipline certainly is needed to attain them.

—Gladys Brooks

*If I go and prepare a place for you,
I will come again and receive you to Myself,
that where I am, there you may be also.*

—JOHN 14:3

□ □ □

No Dead Ends

There is a way which seems right to a man,
but its end is the way of death.

—PROVERBS 14:12

*L*iving in Southern California with all the heavy, unbearable traffic on our freeways, I happen to know a lot of shortcuts that help me to get from point A to point B. With this knowledge, I get a big kick telling out-of-state friends how to take alternate routes that will save them tremendous time in their travel.

As a parent and grandparent we, too, can share alternate routes in life. That is one of the blessings of being more mature in age. We should know more. Throughout life we have observed the wrong routes that people have traveled. We have seen people set out at rush-hour times, and they have lengthened their trips by several hours. We have seen people take the most congested routes that are guaranteed to add more time to their travel. Some people are not very good at following a road map, thus going north when they should have turned south. We have heard about the wrong highways other people have journeyed, or perhaps the foolish routes they have taken, and we know that these roads lead to danger and delays in life.

We want to protect our children and grandchildren from taking the wrong turns in life. They do not have to reinvent the wheel. We have done that for them.

In Christ there is an alternate path that leads them away from the temptations and struggles we may have experienced. Jesus will give them a straight path (Proverbs 3:5-6). Our children and grandchildren are directed by God's Word (Psalm 119:105), and they can experience what a great traveling companion He is (John 8:12).

Our challenge is to model before our children the proper lifestyle so they do not have to travel the road most traveled. They can travel the alternate route of Scripture. In order for us to be able to guide our children in this fashion, we must travel this way ourselves.

Prayer: *Father God, thanks for teaching me the alternate routes in life. You have given me such peace along the way. Fortunately, I am able to travel with You, with fewer delays along the way. Amen.*

Action: Read Proverbs 3:1-12.

Today's Wisdom:

There are three ways that prepare us for life's trials. One is the Spartan way that says, "I have strength within me to do it, I am the captain of my soul. With the courage and will that is mine, I will be master when the struggle comes." Another way is the spirit of Socrates, who affirmed that we have minds, reason and judgment to evaluate and help us cope with the enigmas and struggles of life. The Christian way is the third approach. It does not exclude the other two, but it adds, "You do not begin with yourself, your will or your reason. You begin with God, who is the beginning and the end."

—Lowell R. Ditzen

☐ ☐ ☐

Make a Plan

Those who plan what is good
find love and faithfulness.

—Proverbs 14:22 niv

ou mean I can't just shoot from the hip and hit the moving target? You mean I have to *plan* in order to find success and meet my goals in life? I don't really want to work that hard. I want the easy way out!"

Life does not work that way. If you do not plan, then you plan for failure. None of us wake up in the morning and say, "Today I plan to fail." But, in essence, if we do not plan, that is exactly what we are saying.

The first step for planning is to have a daily planner which goes everywhere with you. It becomes your life. A daily planner is a fantastic tool. "Uh-oh," you might say, "she's talking about planning and organizing again." Well, this is one tool we must discuss because it has made my life so much better. Honestly!

My daily planner almost never leaves my side. I keep an even larger version at home. My home instruction page lists a weekly routine of chores and errands. A quick glance is all I need. Another section is for important numbers—everything from ambulance to veterinarian. Credit cards are listed in another section. You get the idea.

One last tip: The larger notebook is not always convenient, so I keep a daily reminder pad in my kitchen. This daily reminder pad is bright-yellow paper with three columns: "Call," "Do," and "See." Just take an hour or so to invest in setting up your daily planner. It will remove a major cause of stress in your life: disorganization. And you are on the way to a much more organized you!

A great benefit of this planner is you can schedule in personal time and learn to stick with it. After all, just because you plan out your days does not mean that quiet moments cannot be a part of that. Idle time is not hurting you. *Wasted* time is. Life is too precious to spend frivolously or without purpose.

God has given each of us 24 hours a day—no more, no less. One of our family mottos is, "Say no to good things, and save your yeses for the best." In maximizing our time, we have to prioritize the things we do. Do not let every request have the same priority value. You might have Sally call you at the last moment, and she wants you to join her for lunch. This sounds exciting and you would love to do it, but you have already scheduled something of higher priority. So your response must be, "Sorry, Sally, but I have to take a rain check. Thanks for the invitation."

Prayer: *Father God, every day of my life matters! I want each one to count and be significant. Let me seek ways to get the most out of every moment You give me. Amen.*

Action: Say no to some good thing that conflicts with something even more important.

Today's Wisdom:

I have no Yesterdays,
Time took them away;
Tomorrow may not be—
But I have Today.
—Pearl Yeadon McGinnis

□ □ □

You Have Heart Trouble

A wise [woman's] heart guides [her] mouth.

—PROVERBS 16:23 NIV

A couple who have been close friends of ours for many years were having concerns about his difficulty in breathing and a feeling of no energy in his work. The wife (as usual) talked him into seeing his doctor. The day of the appointment came and the diagnosis was not good. The doctors told him, "You have heart trouble." He was in surgery that same afternoon having heart bypass surgery.

"You have heart trouble" are words a patient dreads to hear from the doctor. The fear is that the condition is very serious, or even fatal. Heart defects or heart failure usually occur in men and women past the age of 50, but people of all ages can be affected by heart disease. In fact, my father passed away due to heart failure when I was 11 years old.

Not only do we have a physical heart problem, but we as humans can also have emotional and spiritual heart defects. These can come in many forms. The writer of Proverbs lists six of them:

> ❧ *A deceitful heart*—"Deceit is in the heart of those who devise evil, but counselors of peace have joy" (12:20).

⤳ *A heavy heart*—"Anxiety in a man's heart weighs it down, but a good word makes it glad" (12:25).

⤳ *A sorrowful heart*—"Even in laughter the heart may be in pain, and the end of joy may be grief" (14:13).

⤳ *A carnal heart*—"The backslider in heart will have his fill of his own ways, but a good man will be satisfied with his" (14:14).

⤳ *A proud heart*—"The LORD detests all the proud of heart. Be sure of this: They will not go unpunished" (16:5 NIV).

⤳ *An angry heart*—"The foolishness of man ruins his way, and his heart rages against the LORD" (19:3).

Wrap all of these heart problems together and you have a critical diagnosis. Having even one of the above problems is still very serious. If we find that we have any of these conditions, we must seek help in restoring ourselves to having a good heart unto the Lord. We do not have to go under the knife as in real physical heart bypasses. We can go directly to the Lord, and He will restore our healthy spiritual heart. Confession of our sin is the place to start. My favorite verse is found in 1 John 1:9 which reads, "If we confess our sins, He is faithful and righteous to forgive us our sins and to cleanse us from all unrighteousness." This is a promise that can be taken to the bank. Yes, if you have a spiritual or emotional heart problem, go to the foot of the cross and ask for forgiveness.

Prayer: *Father God, You are a God who can cleanse us from all unrighteousness and make us whole. Thank You for keeping Your promises. Amen.*

Action: Confess your heart problem to the Lord today.
Get rid of it.

Today's Wisdom:

Create in me a clean heart, O God, and renew a
steadfast spirit within me.

—Psalm 51:10

Train Up a Child

❧

In the fear of the LORD there is strong confidence,
and [her] children will have refuge.

—PROVERBS 14:26

ouldn't it be wonderful to send some children to a dog obedience training school (I mean *other* children— not your own, of course, because *our* children are perfect). Our youngest grandchildren recently sent their hyperactive pup to such a trainer. This dog was a nutcase: active, a jumper, a digger, with poor manners. In order for our grand-children and their parents to handle this dog, they had to send it to a dog trainer to help teach this dog proper behavior. Otherwise, they were going to have to sell or give this dog to a good home.

After five weeks and several hundred dollars, this pup returned to their home as a mature, well-behaved dog. All the negatives had been reduced to zero. This trainer was a miracle-worker on their behalf. Now you can visit their home and not be greeted with dirty paws on your chest.

In our culture, we cannot do this type of training for our youngsters, but I have listed a few ideas that may help you in raising your children. Nurturing healthy children includes caring about the simple things that make up a day. I hope some of these ideas will be helpful.

When a child is upset or out of control, try time-outs. This means moving your child to a designated chair or area for a brief period (one minute for every year of age is a good rule) to cool off. It will give the child—and you—a chance to regroup.

Define boundaries and show your child how far he or she may go. Do not hesitate to tell your child, "That is not acceptable behavior in our home." Then share what *is* acceptable. Do not leave your child guessing what is right. Then ask the child to repeat what you said, so that there is no doubt in the child's mind.

Include children—even the youngest—in the housework or the chores around the yard. Make the jobs age-appropriate. For example, an hour of work at a time is about all you can expect from an eight-year-old. Children always respond when there is some reward at the end of the chore. Make it simple—nothing too elaborate.

God wants us to see each one of our children as a delicate rose, eager to unfold its petals to the sun. Remember, once those petals are torn off by harsh words, criticism, or anger, it is almost impossible to put them back on again. Be gentle today, even as the Lord is gentle with you. There are many good Christian-based books on child rearing. Visit your Christian bookstore and ask for recommendations.

Prayer: *Father God, with a child's heart I come to You and surrender myself to You this day. Thank You for Your tenderness and gentleness toward me. You are my life. Amen.*

Action: Try one of the above ideas with your children today.

Today's Wisdom:

    Babies are bits of stardust blown from the hand of God. Lucky the woman who knows the pangs of birth, for she has held a star.

                      —Larry Barretto

Give a Gentle Answer

A gentle answer turns away wrath,
but a harsh word stirs up anger.

—PROVERBS 15:1

I just love the Victorian age of history. The Victorians' clothes, hairdos, makeup, and manners enthrall me. Each time I see a good movie that is set in the latter part of the nineteenth century, my heart longs to return to those days. Back then, women were women and not like the clanging cymbals of today.

I get so unnerved when I hear that certain dress and colors exhibit power in a woman. Where are the days when a woman was known by *who* she was rather than by how much "power" she held over other people?

We women all know that on the inside a woman can be tranquil like the water on Golden Pond, or she can be turbulent like Niagara Falls. This is particularly true when we have disagreements with our mates. At those times, we would do well to heed Solomon's advice in Proverbs 17:14: "The beginning of strife is like letting out water, so abandon the quarrel before it breaks out."

In other words, do not let it start. It is okay to differ with our spouse on an issue, but do not be disagreeable in the process. Keep from speaking in the flesh. Do not let unwholesome words be uttered. Always remember that God often speaks to you through your spouse.

Accept your differences of opinion and grow through these episodes. Conflict when done healthily can be a very constructive experience in a marriage. You can disagree without quarreling.

When we catch ourselves disagreeing, we need to exercise the communication skill of listening, which most of us do very poorly. When we listen, we can begin to better understand the other person's point of view. We all need to be better listeners. Learn to have a quiet and gentle spirit.[9]

One of the most inspiring and challenging verses that can help a couple with their relationship is found in Ephesians 4:29: "Let no unwholesome word proceed from your mouth, but only such a word as is good for edification according to the need of the moment, so that it will give grace to those who hear."

This advice has saved us from many hard feelings. It prevented us from saying words that would harm our relationship. We never have to apologize for words not uttered.

Prayer: Father God, let me protect the words that come out of my mouth. I do not want to be careless in my remarks. May my words be those of encouragement. Amen.

Action: Let no unwholesome words proceed from your mouth.

Today's Wisdom:

A good word is an easy obligation; but not to speak ill requires only our silence, which costs us nothing.

—John Tillotson

□ □ □

Study Your Child

*Train up a child in the way he should go,
even when he is old he will not depart from it.*

—PROVERBS 22:6

This verse deals with dedicating our children to the Lord, which is our religious duty. The verse does not mean to give training for employment or for a professional undertaking. "In the way he should go" means that the education of a child should fit the uniqueness of the individual child. This means we have to be students of our children so we know and understand their individual aptitudes. It also assumes that there be some agreed-upon goal by which "the way" can be defined and measured. This training is truly preparation for life. This means that Mom and Dad must have a plan for raising their children. They cannot be successful if they are just going through life aimlessly.

As we look at our five grandchildren—Christine, Chad, Bevan, Bradley Joe, and Weston—we find ourselves face-to-face with the challenge of understanding each of them so that we can help them develop godly characteristics. We realize that each grandchild is a unique individual with a different style of learning.

In raising our own children, Jennifer and Bradley, we realized that we had to teach, motivate, and discipline each of them according to his or her own unique personality. Through seminars, books, counseling, and Scripture, God helped us understand that children need to be trained in a way tailor-made for them.

In today's verse, Solomon's idea communicates that we parents are to continue training our children as long as they are under our care, and we are to train our children God's way—not according to our ideas or today's popular child psychology.

It is important to see that this verse is not a guarantee to parents that raising our children God's way means that they will never stray from His path. But our efforts to train our children to follow God will be most effective when we use the methods most appropriate to their individual aptitudes and personalities. We need to approach each child differently and not to compare children to each other. We need to be a student of our children. This gives our children a solid, biblical foundation for their lives, and when they are old, they will not depart from it.

Prayer: Father God, please give us as parents insight into each of our children and grandchildren. Help us understand who they are and how best to teach them. Amen.

Action: Learn something new about each one of your children today. Then do something positive with that information.

Today's Wisdom:

Our religion is one which challenges the ordinary human standards by holding that the ideal of life is the spirit of a little child. We tend to glorify adulthood and wisdom and worldly prudence, but the Gospel reverses all this. The Gospel says that the inescapable condition of entrance into the divine fellowship is that we turn and become as a little child. As against our natural judgment we must become tender and full of wonder and unspoiled by the hard skepticism on which we so often pride ourselves. But when we really look into the heart of a child, willful as he may be, we are often ashamed. God has sent children into the world, not only to replenish it, but to serve as sacred reminders of something ineffably precious which we are always in danger of losing. The sacrament of childhood is thus a continuing revelation.

—Elton Trueblood

O Lord,
You have searched me and known me.
You know when I sit down
and when I rise up;
You understand my thought from afar.
You scrutinize my path and my lying down,
And are intimately acquainted
with all my ways.
Even before there is a word on my tongue,
Behold, O Lord, You know it all.

—Psalm 139:1-4

☐ ☐ ☐

A Friend Knows Best

Grievous punishment is for [her] who forsakes the
way; [she] who hates reproof will die.

—PROVERBS 15:10

We often run into people who hate to be disciplined, both children and adults. Someone once stated, "If you do not discipline yourself, you will find someone who will; maybe a coach, a police officer, a drill sergeant—someone will if you don't do it yourself."

Who holds *you* accountable? We all need someone—a husband, a wife, a pastor, a support group, or a friend—to whom we can pour out our deepest heartaches and thoughts. Over the years I have had Bob as my number-one person for accountability. He has helped me to discern how to respond to our children, and now even to our grandchildren. He is my friend, and he is certainly on my team.

If you would ask him, I am sure he would list me as one of his accountable friends. He relies on me to be honest with him when he wants feedback regarding my perception on a speech he has given, on how he relates to his friends, and how he responds to the events of life.

We all have blind spots that need illuminating. If not exposed, they will hinder our spiritual growth. We have to learn to accept loving, caring, constructive criticism. If we are not accountable to another person, we may never understand why people do not feel comfortable around us.

In turn, you can serve in the same role to one of your friends. Do not hedge when someone asks you to be a mentor or to be part of her accountability team. This means the person asking has a lot of confidence in your wisdom and ability to give a straight response when needed.

Prayer: *Father God, thank You for a wise husband and friends who are willing to hold me accountable. Only through their light in my path can I see clearly the way You have for my life. Amen.*

Action: Go to a member of your accounability team and ask that person to shed light on one of your blind spots.

Today's Wisdom:

"You will know the truth, and the truth will make you free" (John 8:32). A virtuous goal for our life is to seek honesty. It might be hard to be honest, but if it is done with loving intentions, the burden of being dishonest will not prevail.

☐ ☐ ☐

A Joyful Heart

A joyful heart makes a cheerful face, but when the heart is sad, the spirit is broken.

—PROVERBS 15:13

The very kernel of joy goes beyond happiness and the circumstances of life. It is the knowledge that *we are loved by God*. We are to rejoice (be full of joy) in God and in each new event He brings into our lives. Psalm 100 (NIV) says we are to:

Shout for joy to the LORD and

- ❧ Worship the LORD with gladness.

- ❧ Come before Him with joyful songs.

- ❧ Know the LORD is God.

- ❧ Know God made us, we are His, we are His people.

- ❧ Know we are the sheep of His pasture.

- ❧ Enter His gates with thanksgiving and His courts with praise.

- ❧ Give thanks to Him and praise His name.

- ❧ Know the Lord is good and His love endures forever.

❧ Know His faithfulness continues through all generations.

What a formula for creating joy in our hearts and a smile on our faces! It is hard to be sad when we accept and acknowledge who we are in Christ.

One of my favorite verses during my long period of illness was Psalm 30:5: "Weeping may endure for a night, but joy cometh in the morning" (KJV). I was able to maintain my joy when I remembered how faithful and unchanging God's character is. When we concentrate and focus on who God is, we have renewed joy. Often my pillow had the wetness of tears early in the evening, but the promise of joy returning in the morning helped dry up my pillow. Each day I would say heartily, "Thank You, Lord, for another good night's sleep and all the excitement of a new day."

Prayer: Father God, when sorrow wants to tug at my heart, reassure me of who You are. Let my face reflect the joy of Your salvation, with smiles of gladness. No frowns allowed today! Amen.

Action: Read Psalm 100 and claim joy for your disposition today.

Today's Wisdom:
The root of faith produces the flower of heart-joy. We may not at the first rejoice, but it comes in due time. We trust the Lord when we are sad, and in due season He so answers our confidence that our faith turns to fruition and we rejoice in the Lord. Doubt breeds distress, but trust means joy in the long run....

Let us meditate upon the Lord's holy name, that we may trust Him the better and rejoice the more readily. He is in character holy, just, true, gracious, faithful and unchanging. Is not such a God to be trusted? He is allwise, almighty, and everywhere present; can we not cheerfully rely on Him?...They that know thy name will trust thee; and they that trust thee will rejoice in thee, O Lord.

—Charles Spurgeon (1834–1892)

If Only

When a [woman] is gloomy,
everything seems to go wrong; when [she]
is cheerful, everything seems right!

—PROVERBS 15:15 TLB

Who wants to be around negative, gloomy people? I know I do not. In America today we meet so many people, and especially teenagers, who have lost all their joy. We are a country full of people who have no hope for the future. When you lose your hope, you soon lose your joy.

We all know that gloom brings doom, but we still seem to concentrate too much on the negative rather than on the positive. Often the glass is seen as half empty rather than being half full. It is all about our attitude toward life. How many times have we said, "If only"?

- If only…I did not have this illness.
- If only…I could win the lottery.
- If only…I had a better job.
- If only…my husband made more money.
- If only…my husband were a Christian.
- If only…my son wouldn't run around with that group of friends.
- If only…my parents were still alive.
- If only…if only…if only.

The negative list could go on endlessly. The "if onlys" of our lives prevent us from being the people God wants us to be. The "if onlys" is a contagious disease. This type of self-pity is never ending. We get caught up in a mindset that prevents us from turning our lives around.

Instead of the gloom, put a little optimism in your life. Memorize Philippians 4:8: "Finally, brethren, whatever is true, whatever is honorable, whatever is right, whatever is pure, whatever is lovely, whatever is of good repute, if there is any excellence and if anything worthy of praise, dwell on these things."

Whenever you are cheerful, everything seems right. Your friends will not stick around if all they hear is, "If only." This kind of conversation drains the life from those around you. "If only" causes you to be friendless, so stop it. Instead of "If only," try "I can."

Prayer: *Father God, I know You do not want to hear my "If onlys." Help me to spread an upbeat attitude and to once and for all bury my negative attitudes. Amen.*

Action: Memorize Philippians 4:8.

Today's Wisdom:

Shout for joy to the LORD, all the earth. Worship the LORD with gladness; come before him with joyful songs. Know that the LORD is God. It is he who made us, and we are his; we are his people, the sheep of his pasture. Enter his gates with thanksgiving and his courts with praise; give thanks to him and praise his name. For the LORD is good and his love endures forever; his faithfulness continues through all generations (Psalm 100 NIV).

Soothing Words Heal

*How wonderful it is to be able to say
the right thing at the right time.*

—PROVERBS 15:23 (TLB)

I guess my tongue has been one of my worst enemies. Over the years I have wished I would not have expressed verbally certain responses to my husband, family, or friends. Not only do I love to say the right thing, I also love to hear the right thing. Pleasant words are pleasing to my ears.

I look to God as my model for communication. He reaches out to us in order for us to have contact with Him. He wants us to initiate contact with Him and with other people. He created us to interact with one another. We were not created to be loners.

The book of Proverbs has good advice on this subject:

- "Some people like to make cutting remarks, but the words of the wise soothe and heal" (Proverbs 12:18 TLB).

- "A good man thinks before he speaks; the evil man pours out his evil without a thought" (Proverbs 15:28 TLB).

- "A word aptly spoken is like apples of gold in settings of silver" (Proverbs 25:11 NIV).

We must be aware of the words we use in our communication. Soothing words heal and build up the hearer. Be on the alert for your selection of words. Pause mentally before speaking to make sure each word expresses what you mean and in such a tone that the other person will receive it in a good spirit. This does not mean you have to be a pushover when serious matters arrive, but you can express your thoughts with proper tone and inflection.

Ask your mate how your style of communication is working in your relationship—what is good and what can be improved.

> No amount of communication can make marriage perfect, and therefore we should not expect it. God is perfect, the ideal of Christian marriage is perfect, and the means God puts at the disposal of Christian couples are perfect. Yet there is no perfect marriage, no perfect communication in marriage. The glory of Christian marriage is in accepting the lifelong task of making continual adjustments within the disorder of human existence, ever working to improve communication skills necessary to this task, and seeking God's enabling power in it all.
>
> —Dwight Small

Healthy relationships must communicate. Many times silence is the worst form of communication. It speaks louder than words. The first step in improving or solving any communication problem is to first realize that there is a problem, and second, to talk about it.

Prayer: *Father God, as You come to me in order for us to fellowship, I realize I must step out of my comfort zone and express in a godly way true love and openness in my communication. Amen.*

Action: Schedule a time with your mate to discuss how you communicate with each other. Remember, there are two parts of communication: listening and talking.

Today's Wisdom:

You may tame the wild beast; the conflagration of the forest will cease when all the timber and the dry wood are consumed; but you cannot arrest the progress of that cruel word which you uttered carelessly yesterday or this morning.

—F. W. Robertson

☐ ☐ ☐

Just You and God

Commit your works to the LORD,
and your plans will be established.

—PROVERBS 16:3

*D*o you have a plan for your life? Without a plan, you will be tossed to and fro. With no plan, you can plan to fail. Most of us just shoot from the hip, hoping we will hit a moving target. God is a God of order. He never intended for us to be confused, with no direction. I have found that if I commit my works to the Lord, I have more clarity in direction for my life.

When was the last time you did something just for you? We all need periods of reappraisal and renewal. We all need time to take stock and take heart. A quiet time gives us the opportunity to identify our most cherished goals and develop ways to achieve them. It also contributes to a sense of inner peace and makes us feel more in control of life. I have found that most people who are disorganized on the outside are first disorganized on the inside. We first have to put our insides in order before we can do anything with our outside disorder.

How do you get started? Let me suggest some tools to help you. The first one is a Bible. Read it daily and get in the habit of going before the Lord in prayer. Scripture tells us to continually be in prayer (1 Thessalonians 5:17). Another helpful tool is to record your prayers, thoughts, and feelings in a journal.

Listen to good music while you write. Take this opportunity to turn off the computer and TV. God wants to speak to our hearts during these quiet times.

Read a good book. I often say that who you will be in five years will be determined by the choices you make, the friends you have, and the books you read. Make activity dates for yourself and pencil them into your calendar. Make sure you keep them. When you make plans, you must remember to write them down and then notice and do them. It does not do any good to write down the appointment but then not read the calendar. Do not miss your appointments. This only creates more stress. Remember, we are trying to reduce stress.

Our crowded schedules and noisy world can make it difficult to take stock of your life. And what do you do about the guilt of taking time for yourself? Get over it.

Prayer: *Father God, I appreciate You reminding me that I must take time for myself if I am going to be an effective wife and mother. Help me to commit my ways unto You. Amen.*

Action: Schedule a quiet time today, just for you and God.

Today's Wisdom:

Good books, like good friends are few and chosen; the more select, the more enjoyable.

—Louisa May Alcott

□ □ □

He Is in Control

The LORD has made everything for its own purpose.

—PROVERBS 16:4

At a recent seminar we attended, the speaker was giving illustrations on control within a family. Some participants thought the actions of various members of a family showed who had control. Comments included:

- The breadwinner of the family has control.
- Mom does because she makes more money.
- The one who signs the checks has control.
- The one who pays the bill at the restaurant when we go out to eat has control.
- The husband has control because he is responsible for the family.

After several more comments were written on the board, a strong male voice in the middle of the audience shouted out, "The one who controls the TV clicker has control!" Everyone laughed, knowing that he was on the right path in most families. Who would ever have thought this statement might really have some validity in our homes? If it is true, then we have lost sight of God's intent for family leadership.

If we are to function as a healthy family, we must realize that God is in ultimate control of our family unit. It takes God and teamwork in order to make things work out in day-to-day living.

Such teamwork leads to confidence in the future. The glue that makes all this happen is the One who will perfect your good work when Jesus returns: the Almighty God. It is so refreshing to know that the possessor of the TV clicker is not ultimately in control. (If it *were* true, I could not have much confidence in what God is capable of doing in my life!)

God is the Potter and I am the clay, and He can do whatever He wishes in my life. In all of life's ups and downs, I do not really need the answer to the question, "Why, God—why me?" Instead, I will be more inclined to ask, "Why *not* me, God?"

Yes, God is in control, and He has done a wonderful job over the centuries. If we are part of His team, we know that we are in good hands. He knows the beginning from the end, and He is more capable of making the right decision than we are.[10]

Prayer: *Father God, over the years I have learned to trust You more. Each time I am tempted to take control of the events of my life, I reflect back over all the things You have decided for me, and they were good. May I always be willing to be the clay and allow You to design me in Your own way. I gladly give my life to You. Thank You for being so dependable. Amen.*

Action: List in your journal four things that you have turned over to God. Share these with a good friend. Request your friend to hold you accountable.

Today's Wisdom:

   I could tell where the lamplighter was by the trail he left behind him.

       —Harry Lauder

☐ ☐ ☐

Keep It Simple

*The mind of [woman] plans [her] way,
but the LORD directs [her] steps.*

—PROVERBS 16:9

*M*any of you who are reading this meditation today are loyal followers and readers of my books on organization. In fact, many of you have even attended my seminars on organization. Maybe you still remember some of my basic principles of organization, but over time you have drifted back to your old disorganized style. Underneath your breath you are calling out, *"Help!"*

Oh, if only life were simpler! Is not this the heart's cry for many of us? Through the years, I have shared with women how important I believe organization is to our peace of mind. Without it, we can never quite find the time we need to do the truly important things.

More Hours in My Day was founded as a ministry to help encourage and teach women how to maximize the minutes and hours of each day, with one purpose in mind: to give them more time with God, family, friends, and community.

Bob and I pray continually that men and women who use our materials will be impacted not only in their homes and lives, but in their spirits as well. Not surprisingly, there seems to be a connection between the two!

Take a moment today to think back over some of the principles for organization we have shared and see if it is time to renew your commitment to put one or more of them into practice today. It is not only having a system that works; you also have to work the system.

Prayer: *Father God, I need to go back to the basics. I need Your help today to implement some things I know I must do to make my life look more like Yours. It is by Your grace, Lord—only by Your grace. Amen.*

Action: Don't pile it; file it.

Today's Wisdom:

Instead of asking yourself whether you believe or not, ask yourself whether you have this day done one thing because He said, *Do it,* or once abstained because He said, *Do not do it!* It is simply absurd to say you believe, or even want to believe, in Him, if you do not do anything He tells you.

—George MacDonald

□ □ □

Pride Comes Before a Fall

*Pride goes before destruction,
a haughty spirit before a fall.*

—Proverbs 16:18 NIV

Candi's dad gave her husband, Vinnie, a Rolex watch. But Vinnie had trouble wearing it because of the weight, size, and discomfort on his wrist. So during the day he would take it off and set it on his desk at work, planning to exchange the watch for something more to his liking as soon as he could. Would you believe that one day when he went to lunch the watch was stolen off his desk? Unfortunately, Vinnie was not able to claim insurance on it even close to its true value.

How mindless, Candi thought. *I cannot believe he was so careless as to leave such an expensive watch lying around on his desk.* She was angry with him about the loss, thinking to herself, *I would never do anything like that.*

A few weeks later Candi was picking up her children at school. In a hurry and distracted by the errands, schedules, and church projects to be done, she mindlessly jumped out of her car, leaving the window down and her purse sitting on the front seat. After collecting her girls and jumping back into the car, away she went. She stopped at a drive-through window to buy a treat for the girls, and—you guessed it—her purse was gone, stolen out of her car in front of the school.

Angry and feeling frustrated with herself, she could not wait to get home and make the calls to credit-card companies. She soon discovered the thief had already charged 500 dollars worth of goods on her cards. Candi began to realize how badly she had treated her husband, when she had done the same kind of careless act as well.

What a great lesson for all of us on treating other people as we want to be treated. That old motto has certainly proven to be true over our years: "What goes around comes around."[11]

Prayer: *Father God, help me to take the log out of my eye before I look for the speck in my friend's eye. Oh, how easy it is to see other people's faults! Let me be reminded to be very careful in all that I do. It only takes a moment of being lax for my world to turn upside down. Amen.*

Action: Take your time as you move through your day. Patience will help you avoid careless mistakes.

Today's Wisdom:

True spiritual maturity, the product of time spent in the Word and continuous walking in the Spirit, manifests itself when Christ's will and your will are synonymous.

—Tim LaHaye

□ □ □

Go Straight to the Source

He who gives attention to the word will find good,
and blessed is he who trusts in the LORD.

—PROVERBS 16:20

When we seek out wisdom, we attach a high priority to wanting to please God by obedience to His Word. I think of knowledge as being horizontal, but wisdom as being a vertical relation between us and God. There are many brilliant individuals who have an encyclopedic brain full of knowledge, but without knowing Jesus they often have little wisdom.

As a child, I often heard my parents say, "Emilie, just use common sense." As I have gotten older, I realize that common sense is not so common anymore. Unless we have a benchmark of God's wisdom, we do not have a reference for using common sense. There are rights and wrongs, and knowledge alone does not always permit us to make good judgments. When we have wisdom, we are able to find good in the fullest sense.

Without wisdom, Charles Spurgeon says, "Man is as the wild ass's colt, running hither and thither, wasting strength which might be profitably employed." Wisdom helps us organize our lives so we do not use a lot of energy wastefully. It is the compass which gives us proper direction for all that comes our way in life. Rather than going down dead-end streets of life, we can be assured that God will give us clear direction. On the compass, north is always north. We can be assured that when God directs us in a certain path, His compass will steer us in the right direction.

You might ask yourself, "Where can we find this wisdom?" Is it something that can be obtained by an ordinary person? Today's reading says that we are to give attention to God's Word, and that we will be blessed if we trust in God. I know that to be a true fact in my life. His wisdom has been able to answer all of my life's big and little concerns. I have found the Bible to be my source of direction. The wisdom I have learned goes far beyond any knowledge that I have been able to acquire in any academic pursuits. The person who trusts in the Lord has a diploma for wisdom. Frame this last sentence and display it on your wall of learning. God never goes back on His promises. If He says it, you can believe that you will receive it. This world is shouting out, "Where are the wise leaders?" Become wise, and you will have people clamoring for your services.

Prayer: *Father God, thanks for letting me go from knowledge to wisdom. Wisdom has served me well over my lifetime. Your wisdom has given me a solid foundation for having common sense. Thank You. Amen.*

Action: Go beyond the horizontal plane of knowledge and begin the vertical relationship of wisdom.

Today's Wisdom:

God has given each of us a purpose for living, and when we are serious about wanting to know it and faithful to obey what He shows us, we can trust Him to guide us into that place of His perfect will.

—Elaine Creasman

☐ ☐ ☐

Follow the Light

There is a way which seems right to a man,
but its end is the way of death.

—PROVERBS 16:25

At one time or another we have come upon a sign that reads, "Dead-end Street." Then we had to turn around, retrace our travel, and head off in a new direction. We looked at our map and expressed our dissatisfaction that it did not show the dead-end street. It looked like it went all the way through.

That is the way it is with us as people. We start out in the right direction, but if we do not watch carefully, we end up in the wrong place. In some instances in Southern California's big cities, you can get into a lot of trouble, even death, if you take the wrong turn and end up in a gang-related neighborhood. Great care should be taken when you start out driving. It could be a beautiful, sunny day, and your gas tank is full as you head out to a great adventure. However, night falls, and you have lost your direction, the gas tank is low, and you are lost. As a last resort, you get off the freeway in a neighborhood that you do not know and you are in *big trouble.*

That is the way it is in real life—particularly with people who have power. When a person exercises power according to his desires, he is likely to abuse it. In the Old Testament, God provided written instructions for ruling Israel. Each king was to personally make a handwritten copy of the Law.

He was to carry this copy of the Law with him and to read it "all the days of his life." This was so that he might learn to:

- ❧ Revere God
- ❧ Obey the Law
- ❧ Not consider himself better than the people he ruled
- ❧ Apply the Law evenhandedly

Even though we are not kings, we do have power over what we say and do. Likewise, I need to pay attention to God's Word throughout the day if I want to exercise this power wisely.

If we listen to the world's ways, we try to achieve the power of money, homes, cars, and prestige. But God's ways are just the opposite. His Word steers me in quite the opposite direction—toward wisdom, compassion, and humility.

If I pay attention to God's Word, it will give me abundance in life; if not, I will head toward death. Very few of us start out the day seeking death, but because of getting away from God's wisdom, we find ourselves being in the wrong place at the wrong time. Let God direct your path with His light, and do not follow the darkness of man.

Prayer: *Father God, let me stay true to Your Word. If I get far away, bring me back from running into a dead-end street. I choose life rather than death. Amen.*

Action: Check your map to see if there are any dead-end streets ahead. If so, turn back before it is too late.

Today's Wisdom:

By going a few minutes sooner or later, by stopping to speak with a friend on the corner, by meeting this man or that, or by turning down this street instead of the other, we may let slip some impending evil, by which the whole current of our lives would have been changed. There is no possible solution in the dark enigma, but the one word "Providence."

—Henry Wadsworth Longfellow

No matter how difficult the way
He promises to hold us steady.

—Author unknown

It Only Takes One

A perverse man spreads strife, and a slanderer
separates intimate friends.

—Proverbs 16:28

From my childhood I have heard, "It only takes one bad apple to spoil the whole barrel," and that is true of people, too. A family, a church, a business is only one person away from turning a good organization into an unhealthy, backbiting, gossiping group of individuals.

In 1520, one person stepped off a Spanish ship in Mexico and caused the deaths of thousand of people. The man was a soldier under the leadership of Pànfilo de Narvàez, and the soldier had smallpox. The soldier did not know it, but wherever he went he exposed the citizens to a new disease. As a result of the ensuing smallpox epidemic, many thousands of Mexicans died.

One man—that is all it took. His contact with the unsuspecting Mexican people led to a horrible, painful scourge. The devastating effects of that disease traveled from one person to another, infecting a large segment of the population.

The spread of any deadly disease is much like the spread of any spiritual sickness that strikes an organization—yes, even the church. Paul addressed this very topic when he wrote to the church of Ephesus about their gossip and unedifying words (Ephesians 4:29-32).

Many times a church can be torn apart because just one person begins to spread gossip among the congregation.

Soon dissension is spread everywhere, and people who used to work together so beautifully are now at each other's throats. The staff has to spend all their time and energy mending fences.

No matter what organization we find ourselves in, we need to be careful not to spread the disease of gossip. As peacemakers we are to use our energy to lift up and encourage those around us. President Truman had a sign on his desk that read, "The buck stops here." That is what we should do when gossip comes our way: Refuse to repeat it. It stops with you.

Prayer: *Father God, give me wisdom to control my tongue. When I hear gossip, let my lips remain shut. Let the buck stop with me. I do not want to pass it on. Amen.*

Action: Read Ephesians 4:29-32.

Today's Wisdom:

Let no unwholesome word proceed from your mouth, but only such a word as is good for edification according to the need of the moment, that it will give grace to those who hear.

—Ephesians 4:29

Living the Life

Grandchildren are the crown of old men,
and the glory of sons is their fathers.

—PROVERBS 17:6

*M*any grandparents have jokingly said that if they would have known grandchildren were so much fun, they would have had them first. Grandchildren give us a chance to be better as grandparents than we were as parents. We bring to the table more maturity, more life experiences, a mellowing-out period of our lives, more time to spend leisurely in conversation, and more financial resources.

In our busy world it is often difficult to slow down and create for young people the kind of moments that we cherish in our own childhood memories. Just as the Lord Jesus always has time for you, take a few extra moments with a little person you love.

At bedtime, tell your grandchildren the beginning of a dream and suggest that they listen with their eyes closed. Before you know it, they will be sound asleep!

Do a project with your children to emphasize how important our treasures can be and to teach them how to protect them. Take a favorite book and cover the front and each page with clear contact paper. It is a simple way to preserve a future heirloom for your children.

Decorate your children's room by having them draw pictures of their favorite activities on butcher paper (brown or white). Then praise them for their handiwork and hang the pictures on the walls around the room.

Read Bible stories to your children and pray with them. It's an important part of their spiritual heritage—one filled with memories they will treasure for a lifetime.

Make a close connection between your family and the older generation (from both sides of the in-laws). There are many ways to stay connected and many traditions you can build into everyone's lives. Work closely with your adult children to complement what values they want to instill in their children. Many times you are able to enrich these experiences because of your position in life. Make it a team effort when working with these precious young ones. Make the golden years golden.

Prayer: *Father God, let me be a creative parent or grandparent as we walk this life with our offspring. You are the Giver of all wisdom. Let me be a student of wisdom and truth. Amen.*

Action: Visit your Christian bookstore and purchase an age-appropriate book as a surprise for your child or grandchild.

Today's Wisdom:

The days may come, the days may go.
But still the hands of memory weave
The blissful dreams of long ago.
—Henry Tucker

What Is a Friend?

A friend loves at all times,
and a brother is born for adversity.

—PROVERBS 17:17

An English publication offered a prize for the best definition of a friend, and among the thousands of answers received were the following:

- ❧ One who multiplies joys, divides grief, and whose honesty is inviolable [kept sacred]
- ❧ One who understands our silence
- ❧ A volume of sympathy bound in a tear towel
- ❧ A watch which beats true for all time and never runs down

And the winner was: "A friend is the one who comes in when the whole world has gone out."

I have been so blessed with great friendships. I know not how I have accumulated so many. At times they remind me of puppies hanging around a food bowl. They each have brought such tenderness to my life and the joy of great anticipation when we meet. Some friends just want to curl up around me and cozy up to a warm blanket and enjoy the strokes I give them. In return, they give me the nudge of their noses that tells me they so enjoy our time together. On occasion, I have even given my friends a time to doze on the couch and awaken again to continue our time together. Friends are so warm and cuddly.

Henry Wadsworth Longfellow once wrote a poem that expressed true love of friends and how they linger over a period of years. It reads:

I shot an arrow into the air,
It fell to earth, I knew not where;
For, so swiftly it flew, the sight
Could not follow it in its flight.

I breathed a song into the air,
It fell to earth, I knew not where;
For who has sight so keen and strong,
That it can follow the flight of a song?

Long, long afterward, in an oak
I found the arrow, still unbroke;
And the song, from beginning to end,
I found again in the heart of a friend.

Prayer: *Father God, what would I do without all my friends? They give me such support and strength. They are what give my day purpose. May I, too, be a friend to my friends. Thank You for friendships. Amen.*

Action: Write a friend a thank-you note for welcoming you into her life.[12]

Today's Wisdom:

The first general rule for friendship is to be a friend, to be open, natural, interested; the second rule is to take time for friendship. Friendship, after all, is what life is finally about.

—Nels F. S. Ferré

Joy in Your Heart

A cheerful heart does good like medicine,
but a broken spirit makes one sick.

—Proverbs 17:22 TLB

My five-year bout with cancer has certainly been a challenge for my joy. I honestly have to say it has been difficult at times. During treatment all patients have ups and all have downs. There are no exceptions. We are not always bumping heaven.

Those of us who are sick certainly do not want to take any more pills, injections, transfusions, or bags of liquid. However, I have found the best medicine of all: joy in my heart. But how do I have joy when I am so sick, even having difficulty keeping food and medicine down? During long periods of treatment, keeping anything down is very problematic.

I must *choose* to have a cheerful heart instead of a broken spirit. Psychologists know from research and case studies that a positive attitude plays a large part in recovery. Our Dr. Barth told us that those patients who have a spiritual dimension seem to go through illness and treatment better than those who do not. Try your best to have a positive attitude daily. Stay out of the dumps, even when your body tells you that you are in the dumps. Be known as a person with a joyful heart. Have a smile for people you meet.

One verse that kept coming to my mind throughout my ordeal (your ordeal might not be sickness, but one of many painful journeys) was found in Psalm 30:5: "Weeping may endure for a night, but joy cometh in the morning" (KJV). Some translations say "a shout of joy." Yes, there are tears, but God also sends shouts of joy in the morning. Be confident in this promise.

Prayer: *Father God, I want to be cheerful today, even when I do not feel like it. Help me to lift my spirits so I can be a blessing to someone who has a special need. I know that when I give a blessing, I receive a blessing. Amen.*

Action: Buy a joke book and read at least one joke a day.

Today's Wisdom:

Laughter is such a part of joy that when it fades in a loved one, our hearts can feel like they are about to break. The return of laughter brings renewed joy.

—Elaine Creasman

God Frowns on Pride

Before destruction the heart of man is haughty,
but humility goes before honor.

—PROVERBS 18:12

merica has become a country of self-centeredness. Everywhere we turn we see me-me-me. The great danger is that we have looked into the pond and seen our reflection. The Greek myth tells us about a beautiful youth who, after Echo's death, is made to pine away for love of his own reflection in a spring and changes into a narcissus (a plant of the lily family, including daffodils and jonquils).

This is where we get the term *narcissism* which is defined by Webster as "self-love; excessive interest in one's own appearance, comfort, importance, and abilities." Regardless where we look, we see pride and arrogance all over, from politicians and movie personnel to sports heroes and business executives. Marketers of products tell us it is all about what we wear, drive, and live in, and where we vacation, what kind of job we have, and the prestige of the school our children attend. When we begin to act out all of this, it makes us appear proud, cocky, and arrogant.

In contrast, if we look at Jesus' life, we see an excellent example of servanthood and humility. He came to serve rather than to be served. All through Scripture we are taught that pride is destructive, but humility has great reward. Jesus never crowed about His greatness. He was willing to serve other people, and even wash their feet. He always demonstrated that we should all be servants to each other and to God.

Several key verses that teach this principle include:

- ⟶ "He has showed you, O man, what is good. And what does the LORD require of you? To act justly and to love mercy and to walk humbly with your God" (Micah 6:8 NIV).

- ⟶ "But all who humble themselves before the LORD shall be given every blessing, and shall have wonderful peace" (Psalm 37:11 TLB).

- ⟶ "Clothe yourselves with humility toward one another, for God is opposed to the proud, but gives grace to the humble. Therefore, humble yourselves under the mighty hand of God, that He may exalt you at the proper time" (1 Peter 5:5-6).

- ⟶ "Humble yourselves in the sight of the Lord, and he shall lift you up" (James 4:10 KJV).

- ⟶ "The humble shall see their God at work for them. No wonder they will be so glad! All who seek for God shall live in joy" (Psalm 69:32 TLB).

Only a life of prayer can help the believer arrive at a spirit of humility, meekness, and Christlikeness.

Prayer: *I am praying, blessed Savior,*
To be more and more like thee;
I am praying that thy Spirit
Like a dove may rest on me.

I am praying, blessed Savior,
For a faith so clear and bright
That its eye will see thy glory
Thro' the deepest, darkest night.

I am praying to be humbled
By the power of grace divine,
To be clothed upon with meekness,
And to have no will but thine.

I am praying, blessed Savior,
And my constant prayer shall be
For a perfect consecration,
That shall make me more like thee.

Chorus:
Thou who knowest all my weakness,
Thou who knowest all my care,
While I plead each precious promise,
Hear, oh, hear and answer prayer.

—Fanny J. Crosby

Action:

Ask God if there is a particular area of your life in which pride has become a problem. Then ask God to show you the way He sees this area of your life.

Today's Wisdom:

A lady once asked her pastor whether a person might not be fond of dress and ornaments without being proud. The minister replied, "When you see the fox's tail peeping out of the hole, you may be sure the fox is within."

☐ ☐ ☐

Be a Listener

He who gives an answer before he hears,
it is folly and shame to him.

—Proverbs 18:13

Every day we read in the newspaper of people who seem to be crying out, "Listen to me, please! Won't someone please stop and hear my cry?" This is a common request from everyone. We are a country of talkers; very few people have the gift of listening.

If you stop and listen very carefully to your conversation at home, your husband and children are making the same cry. Oh, it may not be as loud or theatrical as that of the person in the front-page story, but it is just as real.

When we stop and take time to listen, we are telling the other person, "Your thoughts are important. I care what you think. You have value to me. I want to be involved in your life."

We all have to stop and answer this question: "How good a listener am I?" You will be surprised to know that most of us are not very good with this skill. If we are to love other people, we must be willing to listen to what they have to say. It is impossible to really love people with the love of God and not listen to their thoughts. Marriage matures and goes up another notch when we are able and willing to listen. Marriages do not grow with deaf ears.

Children sometimes complain that their parents do not listen to them, that they are inaccessible. Do your children say this about you? Are you reachable by your children, or must they constantly seek your attention before they get it? And when you finally are available, do you really listen to them?

Here is a test: Would you be satisfied if God listened to you as intently as you listen to your children when they have an urgent request, even if it turns out to be nothing you consider important? When those moments of true listening occur, you need to stop what you are doing, put down the magazine you are reading, turn off the TV, look into the person's eyes, and let that person know he or she has your fullest attention. Do not even answer the phone during these crucial times.[13]

Prayer: *Father God, help me to zip up my mouth when I begin to answer before I listen to find out how the other person yearns to be listened to, especially when it is my child who wants to talk to me. God, You are a parent who is never too busy to listen. May I be the same. Amen.*

Action: Refuse to give an answer before you hear all the facts. No nodding your head "no" is allowed until you have heard it all.

Today's Wisdom:

He who indulges in liberty of speech will hear things in return which he will not like.

—Terence

□ □ □

Being a 2 A.M. Friend

There is a friend who sticks closer than a brother.

—PROVERBS 18:24

Friends and friendships are unique social happenings. Often we wonder why some people are attracted to others. Is it because of common interests, past experiences, physical attractions, having children that are friends with another family's children, or attending the same church? What is it that bonds certain people together?

I have actually had people who have approached me and said, "I would like to be your friend." This can be a difficult request to fulfill. Friendships are not easily made or easily continued. It takes a lot of time and effort to be someone's friend. And it certainly does not happen overnight.

I find that my friends come from various backgrounds, religions, economic levels, and educational achievements. There does seem to be one common strand that runs through most of these friendships: We have a kindred spirit in the Lord. Many of my friends are in various places on their walk with God and in their level of commitment. Some friends are searching, and some are mature in their faith.

The writer of today's proverb gives a warning in the first part of verse 24: "A man of too many friends comes to ruin." When I first read that I was confused. I said to myself, "I thought we were to have a lot of friends. So why this warning?" But as I pondered it, a thought came to me. He was stressing that too many friends chosen indiscriminately will bring trouble, but a genuine friend sticks with you through thick and thin. When we use this criterion for a friend, we begin to thin the acquaintance ranks down to those who are truly our friends. I am fortunate in that all my first-level friends are my "2 A.M. friends," meaning that I could call them at 2 A.M. and they would be by my side at a moment's notice.

You never know when you will need a friend. I have found that those who are friendly have friends. To have friends you must be a friend. Sometimes it takes a special effort to have and to be a friend.

Friendship-making is a skill we need to teach our children. As parents, we have only a short window of opportunity to teach the value of positive friendship. Each year we have less influence on our youngsters because the music, dress, dance, and jewelry selections of the world seem to pull our children from our families. While there is still time, we need to teach our children how to choose the right kind of friends.

Prayer: *Father God, thank You for giving me some wonderful friends. I would not be where I am today without their support and encouragement. Amen.*

Action: Write a friend a note expressing how much you appreciate her friendship.

Today's Wisdom:

A mouse one day happened to run across the paws of a sleeping lion and awakened him. The lion, angry at being disturbed, grabbed the mouse and was about to swallow him when the mouse cried out, "Please, kind sir, I did not mean it. If you will let me go, I shall always be grateful, and perhaps I can help you someday."

The idea that such a little thing as a mouse could help him so amused the lion that he let the mouse go. A week later the mouse heard a lion roaring loudly. He went closer to see what the trouble was and found his lion caught in a hunter's net. Remembering his promise, the mouse began to gnaw the ropes of the net and kept it up until the lion could get free. The lion then acknowledged that little friends might prove great friends.

—An Aesop Fable

All that is good, all that is true, all that is beautiful,
all that is beneficent, be it great or small, be it perfect
or fragmentary, natural as well as supernatural,
more as well as material, comes from God.

—JOHN HENRY NEWMAN

□ □ □

Heart in the Home

He who gets wisdom loves his own soul;
he who keeps understanding will find good.

—PROVERBS 19:8

*I*n another translation we read, "Do yourself a favor and learn all you can; then remember what you learn and you will prosper" (GNT).

These days, we seem to be returning to a new traditionalism. We are looking at our past mistakes and beginning to see what we can do to correct them in order to become the unique women that God created us to be. Yes, we are going back to tradition, but we will do it in a new way. We will take on the mystique of the feminine woman, being a lady for whom men will open doors—not the "too-tired-for-sex" woman, but the woman who is beautiful inside and has charm that a man desires.

How are we going to do this? By changing our values from straw and sticks to gold and silver, and by building a strong foundation of faith in God's Word (1 Corinthians 3:12).

Women, we are the mortar that holds together our homes and families. We set the spiritual thermostat in our homes. Proverbs 14:1 says that homes are made by the wisdom of women but are destroyed by foolishness. Yes, we have been foolish in some areas. We have grown and learned, and now we are ready to commit ourselves to making positive changes.

Heart in the home is created by teaching, delegating, and being there. We need to be there for our families. When Jenny, our daughter, got a splinter, had a fever, tried out for the swim team, was rejected by friends, had hair that did not fall right, broke up with a boyfriend, and planned her wedding—I was there.

My mother became a single parent after my father died. She worked far into the night, and during all her years until she died at age 78, she remained the heart of our home. Through all the abuse, alcohol-related problems, low finances, and anger in our home, Mama remained a soft, gentle-spirited woman. During her later years she lived in a senior-citizen building in a tiny efficiency apartment. Yet she had a wreath of flowers on her front door and a few fresh daisies or pansies on the table, and she always had a cup of tea ready for anyone who knocked.

What can we do to repair the brokenness of our home, hearts, health, marriage, relationships, and children? We can begin by looking at the 8760 hours we have each year and reducing the 70 percent of stress in our lives that is caused by disorganization. If we sleep an average of eight hours per day, that equals 2920 hours a year. We then work about 2000 hours, which give us 3840 hours to wash, iron, plan and prepare food, clean, attend Little League or soccer games or music recitals, keep doctor appointments, help with homework, and watch television. About 37 hours a week is what it takes to accomplish our domestic chores. If we work outside our homes, how can we be there to do all that? There is no time left for us or for any interaction with our family.

Women, we are the remodelers, the harmonizers of our homes. We are a country of broken homes, broken hearts, and broken health. Staying married today is more of a challenge than getting married. To keep the flame of love alive takes creative work. Several things need to happen:

❧ Submit one to another (Ephesians 5:21).

❧ Make your mate feel special.

❧ Be willing to follow the leadership of your husband. You have important input in that leadership. For him to lead, there must be a follower.

❧ Shower your mate with love.

❧ Respect your mate.

Receive or rededicate yourself to Christ. Be an active part of the family of God, and then wait and allow God to work in your family.[14]

Prayer: *Father God, thank You for choosing me to be the heart of our home. By nature that is my love. I get so excited when I see how my family responds to all that I do. Yes, there are times when I have to ask for a thank-you, but thank You for giving me a husband, children, and grandchildren who respond in such a positive fashion when I do my mother things. I know I have made a positive impact when I see my children, Jenny and Brad, do some of the same things in their homes. May those women reading today's thoughts step out in a new way. Amen.*

Action: *Delegate.* Women, we cannot do it alone. Supermom must go out the window. Call a family meeting and share with them your need for help and how they can help you. I know your family will come through. Prepare ahead of time a list of areas in which they can relieve some of the stress from your life.

Today's Wisdom:

Continue to share your stress feelings and allow your family to share with you. As busy as we all are, it is important to communicate back and forth about our feelings concerning teachers, schoolwork, friends, and (especially) God.

Though I am not what I ought to be,
nor what I wish to be,
nor yet hope to be, I can
truly say I am not what I once was,
a slave to sin and Satan.

—John Newton

A Look at Anger

Good sense makes a man restrain his anger,
and it is his glory to overlook a
transgression or an offense.

—PROVERBS 19:11 AMP

nger burns like a hot brushfire. As I read my daily newspaper and view the TV news, I am constantly reminded of the sin of anger. Not a day goes by when the media does not report the sad results of anger: murder, road rage, drunk driving, gang warfare, arson fires, child beating, rape, etc.

A healthy relationship cannot exist where anger exists. The two do not go together. In order for friendships to flourish, we must be able to control this raging fire that exists in most human beings. The book of Proverbs gives some insight concerning anger. These passages are all from *The Living Bible:*

- "A short-tempered man is a fool. He hates the man who is patient" (14:17).

- "A quick-tempered man starts fights; a cool-tempered man tries to stop them" (15:18).

- "It is better to be slow-tempered than famous; it is better to have self-control than to control an army" (16:32).

❧ "A fool gets into constant fights. His mouth is his undoing! His words endanger him" (18:6-7).

❧ "A short-tempered man must bear his own penalty; you can't do much to help him. If you try once you must try a dozen times!" (19:19).

❧ "Keep away from angry, short-tempered men, lest you learn to be like them and endanger your soul" (22:24-25).

❧ "A rebel shouts in anger; a wise man holds his temper in and cools it" (29:11).

❧ "There is more hope for a fool than for a man of quick temper" (29:20).

❧ "A hot-tempered man starts fights and gets into all kinds of trouble" (29:22).

❧ "Anger does not make us good, as God demands that we must be" (James 1:20).

If anger is one of your enemies, go to God in prayer and ask for healing. It is a disease like cancer and can destroy your body if not addressed. Do not wait until it is too late. Healthy relationships demand that anger be conquered.

Prayer: *Father God, let me examine myself to see if there is any evidence of anger. If so, I want to give it to You. May You help me conquer this dragon that wants to destroy me. Amen.*

Action: Examine yourself to see if there is any anger in your soul.

Today's Wisdom:

> I am naturally as irritable as any; but when I find anger, or passion, or any other evil temper arise in my mind, immediately I go to my Redeemer; and confessing my sins, I give myself up to be managed by him.

> —Adam Clarke

Confidence—
"I will fear no evil."

—H. A. IRONSIDE

□ □ □

Keep Eyes and Ears Alert

Discipline your son [or daughter]
while there is hope.

—PROVERBS 19:18

As parents we must be ready for every teaching opportunity. Our eyes and ears must be open and focused on those events that surround us and our children. When we see or hear infractions of God's principles, we must be willing and able to discipline in a loving way. If we forget to discipline at an early age and let one misbehavior slide by, then another, and another, we will not be able to discipline when the big infraction comes.

A good example of such a teaching moment was shared by a friend of mine. My friend recalls that her three-year-old daughter had been visiting the older girl next door. They were joyfully playing a game of jacks, and all of a sudden the ball bounced behind a piece of outdoor furniture. Upon trying to retrieve the errant ball, the girl spotted a magic tool: a hammer like her dad's. Her little friend saw her interest in the hammer and told her, "It's no good. It's broken."

But the hammer looked very desirable to my friend's daughter. Her daddy could fix it up like new. She had watched him repair all kinds of broken tools in the past. She knew he could do it. So without a second thought, the little girl took it home (after all, the older girl did not want the hammer because the handle was broken). There was one problem: The little daughter did not ask permission to take the hammer home. My friend was watching as her little daughter was returning home from this short 30-minute visit to her friend's jack game.

As the mom saw this broken hammer in her little girl's hand she asked, "And what do you have in your hand?" The little daughter replied, "Oh, it's an old hammer that has a broken handle." This led to a discussion about how she acquired the hammer. After a short discussion, Mom realized that the hammer was taken without permission from her friend. The girl stated, "Anyway, nobody saw me take it."

Mother very gently put the little girl on her lap and told her about other people's property rights in a language she understood. Then my friend said very gently, "God saw you." With continued discussion, the little girl and her mother returned the broken hammer to her friend.

What a day of learning for both my friend and her daughter. Mom had seized upon this learning opportunity to teach a valuable lesson to her daughter.

Prayer: *Father God, keep my eyes and ears wide open so I can be attuned to the actions around me. When I see a violation of God's law, may I very lovingly use this as a teachable moment.*

Action: Be prepared to correct when correction is needed.

Today's Wisdom:

I will do my best to be
honest and fair,
friendly and helpful,
considerate and caring,
courageous and strong, and
responsible for what I say and do,

and to
respect myself and others,
respect authority,
use resources wisely,
make the world a better place, and
be a sister to every Girl Scout.

—*Junior Girl Scout Handbook*

"For I know the plans that I have for you,"
declares the Lord,
"plans for welfare and not for calamity
to give you a future and a hope."

—JEREMIAH 29:11

Hurry Up, God

The fear of the LORD leads to life, so that one may
sleep satisfied, untouched by evil.

—PROVERBS 19:23

leep disorder is one of America's manifestations for all the stress in our lives. Each of us has our own theories of why we do not sleep well: caffeine, chocolate, eating too late, working too hard, worries, finances, marriage problems—on and on. The tossing and turning are terrible. If our bodies do not get the right kind of sleep, we are going to have many other problems. Tired bodies cannot meet the demands of the day.

I want God to work everything out...*now!* Don't you sometimes feel this way, too? Maybe your child is having trouble at home or at school. Maybe you are worried about an upcoming commitment you made. Maybe you are anxious about your circumstances.

I can tell you what works for me when I grow tired and impatient about life. I read God's Word. Psalm 69:17-18 says, "Do not hide from me, for I am in deep trouble. Quick! Come and save me. Come, Lord, and rescue me" (TLB). The truth of the matter is that God will rescue me, but in His time and not by my hurried pace. I find that God's clock runs slower than my watch. In fact, while I am fretting about not receiving help, maybe help is already on the way or within easy reach. I just have to trust His timing and commitment to me, His child. He hears my cries and sees my tears. I certainly appreciate God's loving patience with me in the midst of the process.

Father God, slow me down. You are great and awesome. Let me not major on the minors but upon the larger issues of life.

Prayer: *Father God, let me rest content. As I enter sleep tonight, give me Your blessing of peace and tranquility. You know my body needs the rest. Amen.*

Action: Set the kitchen timer for five minutes. Spend the time in absolute quiet and stillness.

Today's Wisdom:

The storm was raging. The sea was beating against the rocks in huge, dashing waves. The lightning was flashing, the thunder was roaring, the wind was blowing; but the little bird was sound asleep in the crevice of the rock, its head tucked serenely under its wing. That is peace: to be able to sleep in the storm! In Christ we are relaxed and at peace in the midst of the confusions, bewilderments and perplexities of this life. The storm rages, but our hearts are at rest. We have found peace—at last!

—Billy Graham

Guard Your Promises

A righteous [woman] who walks in [her]
integrity—how blessed are [her] sons after [her].

—Proverbs 20:7

My Bob often says, "Just do what you say you are going to do!" This has been our battle cry for more than 30 years. People get into all sorts of problems because they forget to keep their promises. It is so easy to make a verbal promise for the moment, and then grapple with the execution of that promise later.

Sometimes we underestimate the consequences of not keeping the promise flippantly made in a moment of haste. Many times we are not even aware that we have made a promise. Someone says, "I'll call you at 7:00 tonight," or "I'll drop by before noon," or "I'll call you to set up a breakfast meeting on Wednesday." Then the weak excuses begin to follow. "I called but no one answered" (even though you have an answering machine and no message was left). "I got tied up and forgot." "I was too tired."

I suggest that we do not make promises if we are not going to keep them. The person on the other end would prefer not hearing a promise that is not going to be kept. Yes, there will be times when the execution of a promise will have to be rescheduled, but be up-front with the person when you call to change the time frame. We are not perfect, but we can mentor proper relationship skills to our friends and family by exhibiting accountability with our words of promise. We teach people that we are trustworthy, and how they can be trusted, too.

You will be surprised how people will pleasantly be surprised when you keep your promises. As my friend Florence Littauer says, "It takes so little to be above average." When you develop a reputation for being a woman who does what she says, your life will have more meaning, and people will enjoy being around you.[15]

Prayer: *Father God, I want to be a woman that other people can trust when I make a promise. Let me examine my words to make sure I only give promises when I am committed to fulfilling what I have uttered. Truly, keeping promises reflects on my Christian witness. Convict me to be true to my words. Amen.*

Action: Carry out today the promises you made yesterday.

Today's Wisdom:

A person of integrity knows the difference between right and wrong and with great effort chases after doing right, no matter what hurdles lie ahead. Strive to live a life above reproach.

Push In and Wait

Wait for the LORD, and He will save you.

—PROVERBS 20:22

Learning to wait is one of the most difficult things to learn. I know that my schedule says, "Hurry, hurry, hurry." I did that for the past two decades, and the Lord kept telling me to slow down. I would answer Him, "I will when I get finished with this or that." One year led to another, and another led to another and God kept saying, "Slow down." After repeatedly listening to me making promises and breaking them, God one day said, "That is it. I have told you to slow down, and you haven't heeded My advice."

In 1997 I was diagnosed with cancer and spent the next seven years slowing down. In fact, there was a period of time when I came to a screeching halt. I was not able to advance to Go or collect 200 dollars.

Through this time span I learned to wait on doctors, nurses, tests, and test results, while going from one specialist to another. It seemed like Bob and I were waiting all the time. It was like that old military saying, "Hurry up and wait." Wait, wait, wait. All we did was wait.

There was a good story that a teacher friend told me concerning this very concept of waiting. One of her young students was stuck in an elevator and did not know how to get the elevator moving, and my friend became concerned about the child's safety. This was a child who had

difficulty reading. My teacher friend had spent consider-
able time teaching her student how to unlock words by
breaking them into small pieces. After the student was res-
cued, the small child told the teacher that she had sounded
out *push*.

"I knew I had a *p* which had a puffing sound, and the
u was short and sounded like 'uh' between two consonants
and *sh* is the shushing sound. I already knew the words
button and *in*. So I pushed the button in, and I knew
someone would help me."

As my friend sat down and reflected on this student's
situation, she knew that this child had reinforced a very
valuable lesson in life: When you are in a difficult situation, you push the button and wait.

When she told me this real-life story, I remarked to my
friend, "She is right. I must learn to push the button and
wait!" That is what I have learned through this most difficult time of my life. Push the button and wait. Someone
will come along and help me out of my situation.

God has an unusual way of making us slow down, but
I am still learning it. I certainly do not want to get back into
the same rat race. He has my full attention.

Prayer: *Father God, may we all learn to push the button
in and wait for You to come to our rescue. I am
amazed that You are concerned for even me—
Your child. I have learned to wait the hard way,
but I am ready for my promotion to the next level
of life. Amen.*

Action: Listen to God when He says, "Slow down."

Today's Wisdom:
                Waiting,
                endless waiting.

Why does it seem impossible
to wait patiently
and
graciously—
for the overdue phone call
or the long-expected letter...
for delayed company to arrive
or a sick loved one to get better?

Is there a special ingredient
to fill the waiting time
and ease the heavy burdens
that weigh upon my mind?

Could waiting possibly achieve a work
which nothing else can do?
God, teach me how to
wait patiently
and put full trust
in You.

                              —Author Unknown

□ □ □

Learn to Learn

Since the LORD is directing our steps,
why try to understand everything
that happens along the way?

PROVERBS 20:24 TLB

I do not know about you, but I give everything to God and then, when He is not moving fast enough, I have a tendency to take back the control so I can speed things up. Human nature makes me want to know the answers to so many questions before I step out in faith. When am I going to get it? At times I feel like the disciples when they kept asking Jesus all of their questions. I often say, "They do not get it." I am sure Jesus looks down on me and says the same thing: "Emilie, you do not get it."

One of my recent big questions was, "But God, are You sure that You meant this disease for me? Didn't You mean for it to go to someone else? I am sure You made a mistake when You gave me this illness." Does that kind of thinking sound familiar?

I know it crossed my mind once or twice. I honestly did not want to accept the diagnosis of cancer. Other people get this sickness, but not me.

However, after I got over the shock, and my emotions and thought process came back to earth, I knew I had two choices: be angry at God, or accept what I was about to go through and realize that this situation was going to make me more complete in Christ. Trials are never wasted, nor

196

does God ever give them to the wrong person. Trials are growth hormones for our Christian walk. They develop us into persevering believers. We are stronger coming out of the situation than when we first entered it.

God did not give me cancer, but He did give me the opportunity to grow as a person during this adventure. Through all the pain, tears, hurts, inconveniences, and prayers, I learned to grow and depend upon His Word. Yes, we grow and learn as we cry and pray.

Prayer: *Father God, I want to open my heart and learn from the trials I have; however, I struggle at times. My natural self wants to resist these trials. Thank You for understanding my humanness. Amen.*

Action: Learn to lean on God's promise that He will direct your paths.

Today's Wisdom:

Don't Quit

When things go wrong, as they sometimes will,
When the road you're trudging seems all uphill,
When the funds are low and the debts are high,
And you want to smile but you have to sigh,
When care is pressing you down a bit,
Rest if you must, but don't you quit.

Life is strange with its twists and turns
As every one of us sometimes learns;
And many a failure turns about
When he might have won had he stuck it out.
Don't give up though the pace seems slow;
You may succeed with another blow!

Success is failure turned inside out,
The silver tint of the clouds of doubt;
And you never can tell just how close you are,
It may be near when it seems so far.
So stick to the fight when you're hardest hit;
When things seem worst, you must not quit.

—Author Unknown

Save Little by Little

*Wise people live in wealth and luxury, but stupid
people spend their money as fast as they get it.*

—Proverbs 21:20 GNT

If we took all the wealth in America and distributed it to the poor, within 20 years the wealthy would be wealthy again and the poor would be poor. Why is that? Because most wealthy people know and understand the basic principles of money, and most poor people do not.

One of the hardest principles to teach and to grasp is financial discipline. We in America are a nation of spenders and consumers, and most of us know little about the importance of saving. To be financially independent, we must spend less than we make.

Thomas Stanley in his book *The Millionaire Mind* states, "The success of the millionaire is due to his discipline and has little to do with luck or happenstance. It is hard to overemphasize the importance of discipline in accounting for variation in economic success."

There are many Christian books that can help you establish the discipline to become financially independent, but the bottom-line principles include:

- Save little by little.

- Say no to consumable goods that are not necessary.

⌐ Develop a plan for saving.

⌐ Spend less than you make.

⌐ Use credit cards only if you pay off the balance at the end of each month.

⌐ Give to the Lord's work on a weekly basis.

⌐ Never gamble or play the lottery.

⌐ If it sounds too good to be true, it probably is.

⌐ Never buy anything from a solicitor over the phone.

⌐ Go into a career you are passionate about.

⌐ Choose a market niche that few people are trying to fill.

⌐ Be willing to take a risk after prayer and wise counsel.

⌐ Believe in yourself and your product.

⌐ Think success, not failure.

⌐ Be thankful to God for the opportunity He has given you.

Prayer: *Father God, I truly want to learn Your principles for financial success. Help me to be financially responsible with all You have given me. Amen.*

Action: Read a good book on developing a financial plan. Learn all you can about finance. Set your goals and work very hard at attaining these goals.

Today's Wisdom:

I never did anything worth doing by accident, nor did any of my inventions come by accident, they came by work.

—Thomas A. Edison

∽

*Don't let what you cannot do
interfere with what you* can *do.*

—JOHN WOODEN

∽

☐ ☐ ☐

Build with Words

A soothing tongue is a tree of life,
but perversion in it crushes the spirit.

—Proverbs 15:4

How do you convey your love or dislike to someone: through your eyes, your body language, looks you give, what you do, or what you say? All of these manifestations are called communication—verbal and nonverbal. The strength of our marriage depends on how we communicate. Your marital strength will come from the honesty you and your mate have in communication.

Communication is like a bridge which lets us cross over into another's territory. Words are a very powerful way in which we express acceptance or rejection. Soothing words are delightful and give the speaker and hearer life. Harsh words are rejected and tear down the bridge by which we cross over to another person. We want to be very careful with the words we choose. One of my favorite passages that has given our family many guidelines is found in Ephesians 4:29: "Let no unwholesome word proceed from your mouth, but only such a word as is good for edification according to the need of the moment, so that it will give grace to those who hear." Whenever conversation got offbeat, another member of the family would ask, "Is that edifying?" That is all it took for us to get back on track. We halted the tearing-down conversation and began to build up.

Words That Build Up	Words That Tear Down
You look beautiful.	Shape up or ship out.
Your hair is pretty.	Comb your hair.
Your room is tidy.	Your room is a mess.
Your report card was good.	Don't be so stupid.
This was a good dinner.	Leftovers again?
You keep the home tidy.	This home is a mess.
You are a frugal shopper.	You waste so much money.
You love the Lord.	You never go to church.
I'm sorry.	Out of the way!
I'm excited for you.	You disappoint me so much.
You bring me happiness.	You make me sad.
I feel accepted around you.	You never compliment me.
I thank the Lord for you.	I wish you were never born.
I like being around you.	I can't stand you.

We do not build someone up by tearing that person down. Be very careful in how you word your statements. Put yourself in the other person's shoes. Would you like to be talked to like that?

When we are good communicators, we are better listeners than talkers. Our society has lost the skill of being good listeners. We all want to speak our minds. One of the best ways in which to communicate is to ask the other person a question like:

- ∽ Tell me about...

- ∽ I would like to hear what you think about...

- ∽ What did you see?

- ∽ Tell me what you heard.

- ∽ What do you like about...

These invitation questions give the other person an opportunity to tell you thoughts and opinions in his or her own style and way. You are not controlling the dialogue. Guard your conversation! When you leave, let the other person express that it was good talking to you. I have found that people love to talk about themselves. They are much more excited to talk about their interests than yours, so give them the opportunity.

Prayer: Father God, let me use good words that build bridges among my family and friends. Hold me accountable to using only healthy words—words that edify. Amen.

Action: Examine the words you use. Do they give life, or do they bring death?

Today's Wisdom:

The world is a looking-glass, and gives back to every man the reflection of his own face. Frown at it, and it in turn will look sourly at you; laugh at it, and with it, and it is a jolly, kind companion.

—William M. Thackeray

It Is Okay to Be Strict

Foolishness is bound up in the heart of a child;
the rod of discipline will remove it far from him.

—PROVERBS 22:15

"Strict parent" is not a very good phrase to use at social gatherings today. From my observations of some children raised in the church, it is not even politically correct within the confines of *that* institution! We can easily observe in a child's behavior if his or her parents have limitations within the confines of their home.

One of the easiest tip-offs on this topic is to see with what respect the child speaks to his or her parents. Many children today show little respect when addressing the adults in their lives, whether teacher, coach, policeman, pastor, or parent. When we see such behavior, we know that these children come from a home that is not strict.

In all types of situations we read or hear about the sad results when a child is allowed to roam without any boundaries. One of the saddest results is when we hear of a child losing his or her life because he was never required to heed the warning of a parent. What a tragedy when a senseless death occurs because a child has never learned to obey! *No* is such a simple word, but so difficult to obey.

The world has painted the word *strict* as meaning child abuse and robbing a child of his free spirit so he will not become himself. But in reality, *strict* is a word that develops focus, discipline, achievement, peace, balance, and success in life.

As our children, Brad and Jennifer, have become older, they thank us for giving them boundaries when they were in their formative years. They knew that Mom and Dad loved them, were affectionate to them, verbally praised them, and emotionally supported them. In fact, in many areas of child-rearing, our children are stricter with their own children than we were with them.

Several years ago the Houston, Texas, police department sponsored a large public-relations campaign to combat the rising tide of juvenile crime. Chuck Swindoll in his book *You and Your Child* relates one of the most effective messages in this campaign: "Twelve Rules for Raising Delinquent Children":

1. Begin with infancy to give the child everything he wants. In this way he will grow up to believe the world owes him a living.

2. When he picks up bad words, laugh at him. This will make him think he's cute.

3. Never give him any spiritual training. Wait until he is 21 and then let him "decide for himself."

4. Avoid the use of *wrong*. He may develop a guilt complex. This will condition him to believe later, when he is arrested for stealing a car, that society is against him and he is being persecuted.

5. Pick up everything he leaves lying around. Do everything for him so that he will be experienced in throwing all responsibility on others.

6. Let him read any printed matter he can get his hands on. Be careful that the silverware and drinking glasses are sterilized, but let his mind feast on garbage.

7. Quarrel frequently in the presence of your children. In this way they won't be so shocked when the home is broken up later.

8. Give a child all the spending money he wants. Never let him earn his own.

9. Satisfy his every craving for food, drink, and comfort. See that his every sensual desire is gratified.

10. Take his part against neighbors, teachers, and policemen. They are all prejudiced against your child.

11. When he gets into real trouble, apologize for yourself by saying, "I could never do anything with him."

12. Prepare for a life of grief. You will be likely to have it.[16]

You and your spouse need to decide today what effects you want to have on your children. Also remember that how they live today is more than likely how the next three generations will live. It is up to us as parents to stand in the gap and hang tough. This is not an easy battle, for the evil one would like you to give in to the path of least resistance, but you must be willing to take the "road less traveled."[17]

Prayer: *Father God, thanks for encouraging me today that being strict is okay and that the pressure I receive from other people means I am doing a good job in establishing the boundaries in our home. I wish there were an easier way to raise well-behaved children, but I see that there are not any. I appreciate Your giving to me a caring attitude so that I am motivated to endure all the backlash. I ask that You put into the hearts of my children a sense of obedience to authority. I so very much want them to care. Please put a protective hedge around their little lives. Amen.*

Action: Each day for the next two weeks meet with your
spouse and review one of the 12 rules to see how
you are doing in each area.

Today's Wisdom:

Children have never been very good at listening
to their elders, but they have never failed to imitate them.

—James Baldwin

□ □ □

Having Heart Knowledge

Incline your ear and hear the words of the wise,
and apply your mind to my knowledge.

—PROVERBS 22:17

One of the advantages of growing old is that people perceive you as being wise. Our grandson Chad refers to his Papa Bob as being the wisest man he knows. Imagine that coming from a teenager. What a compliment! However, that wisdom does not come from head knowledge as much as it comes from heart knowledge—that which come from God's Word.

The older I become, the more I realize that living from my heart has value. Let's spend some mellow moments together—no decorating, no organizing...just heart-to-heart. I would like to share what I have learned from my own time with God.

I want to live a life that is meaningful to my family and me. I want my decisions to be based on my Christian values. I do not want my decisions based on convenience, pressure, or selfishness. And in order to do that, I have to have some quiet time to read and think. Do you give yourself room and time to just be quiet? It is amazing how even 15 minutes of peace and reflection can renew your spirit.

When life becomes too hectic, when I am constantly rushed, there is an inner disturbance that prevents me from making well-thought-out decisions. My personal growth grinds to a halt. My prayer is, "Father God, let me be more aware of the feelings of my heart. Let me gain my wisdom from Your precious Word. Keep me on track and let me separate the world's thoughts from Your thoughts." Here is a simple question for you today: "How do you really want to live your life?" Begin today to act upon your answer to this question. In fact, for your next few quiet times or moments of devotion, I encourage you to revisit this question. Journal, pray, or just sit and ponder this question. Your priorities will become very clear as God's priorities become your own.

Surround yourself with godly people who can give you sound scriptural counsel in time of need. Do not be swayed by what the world tells you, but go directly to the "Owner's Manual," the Holy Bible. This counsel will give you great wisdom and a benchmark for what is *truth*.

Prayer: *Father God, how should I live my life? I want my faith to guide my decisions. I want to be calm and clear-thinking in situations so that I can follow Your priorities for my life. Amen.*

Action: Find wisdom for your heart today in God's Word.

Today's Wisdom:

If any of you need wisdom, you should ask God, and it will be given to you. God is generous and won't correct you for asking. But when you ask for something, you must have faith and not doubt. Anyone who doubts is like an ocean wave tossed around in a storm. If you are that kind of person, you cannot make up your mind, and you surely cannot be trusted. So do not expect the Lord to give you anything at all.

—James 1:5-8 CEV

The Power of Words

For as [she] thinks within [her]self, so [she] is.

—PROVERBS 23:7

In America today, we have lost the power of words. Each year, our "dumbing down" culture enjoys debasing the English language. The entertainment media seem to get a great thrill in seeing how low they can get before parents say, "Stop—that's enough!" Words are powerful, and their proper use should be upheld.

An English professor once said, "Develop a rich vocabulary, for without the right language, the soul is impoverished." This professor was correct. Words shape our thoughts, thoughts shape our attitudes, and attitudes shape our will.

From junior and senior high school, I can remember several English teachers who stressed the importance of thinking before speaking. These instructors stressed the importance of selecting the correct words when speaking and writing. A misused word can be as faulty as an improperly placed decimal point. These English teachers promoted vocabulary development in their students and a love for the written and spoken word.

As women of God, we need to be disciplined in the words we use. Not only is this proper, but it also determines who we are and whom we are becoming. Let's not limit ourselves by not being able to express ourselves properly.

211

When we discipline our use of words, we allow God to fill our minds with wholesome thoughts that influence our destiny.

Prayer: *Father God, let me not forget the power in words. I want to be a learner—a person who disciplines what goes in my eyes, through my brain, and out of my mouth. Amen.*

Action: Today guard the words that you use, and make sure that they are proper for the occasion.

Today's Wisdom:

Finally, brethren, whatever is true, whatever is honorable, whatever is right, whatever is pure, whatever is lovely, whatever is of good repute, if there is any excellence and if anything worthy of praise, dwell on these things.

—Philippians 4:8

Stop Means Stop

Apply your heart to discipline,
and your ears to words of knowledge.

—PROVERBS 23:12

When a child is allowed to roam without any boundaries, tragedy usually follows. One of the saddest results is when a child loses his or her life because the parents never established the discipline of authority and respect.

A family had taken shelter in the basement as a severe storm passed over their town. The radio warned that a tornado had been spotted. When the storm had passed by, the father went upstairs and opened the front door to look at the damage. A downed power line was whipping dangerously on the street in front of their house. Before the father realized what was happening, his five-year-old daughter ran right by him, headed for that sparkling wire in the street.

"Laurie, stop!" he yelled. Laurie just kept going.

"Laurie, stop!" Laurie ran right for the enticing cable.

"Stop now, Laurie!"

Little Laurie reached down to pick up the wicked power line and was instantly killed.[18]

What a heartbreaking tragedy! But the real tragedy is that this happened because a little girl had never been taught that when her father said no, he really meant it. It cost him the life of his daughter.

One of the roles we have as parents is to be teachers. We should continually be on the lookout for situations that afford us the opportunity to teach our children. If we do, our children will be able to hear and heed our commands, knowing we have knowledge and their best interest in mind. How we train our little ones today is more than likely how the next three generations will live.

It is up to us, as parents, to stand in the gap and hang tough. This is not an easy battle (and it is truly a battle), for the evil one would like us to give in to the path of least resistance. We must be willing to travel the road less traveled, even if it entails conflict and discipline.[19]

Prayer: *Father God, give us humble hearts and the determination to teach our children godly principles. When they hear instruction, help them respond in a positive way. Amen.*

Action: Instruct your children so they will hear your words of knowledge. Role-play a similar situation to the one above when you have to give out a command to "Stop!"

Today's Wisdom:

Who among you is wise and understanding? Let him show by his good behavior his deeds in the gentleness of wisdom.

—James 3:13

Share Your Life in Pictures

Let your father and your mother be glad,
and let her rejoice who gave birth to you.

—Proverbs 23:25

Nothing is better in life than to have Mom and Dad happy to be your parents. There is something about their approval that places it at the top of a child's list. Far too often this cannot be said because of various incidents that happened in childhood, where either the parents were disappointed because of their children's behavior, or the children were disappointed because of their own parents' behavior.

If we have not had a pleasant experience either as a parent or as a daughter of imperfect parents, we can say, "The buck stops here. We are going to have a new beginning." So how do we repair or establish new relationships? Begin to honor those who have come before.

Collections of any kind are usually a way for people to share stories and honor people. Do you collect teacups or spoons or stuffed animals? If so, I bet you can share with any visitor where you got each and every one or who gave you a particular one as a birthday gift four years ago.

Have you ever thought of your family photos as a collection that can honor people? By gathering together these special treasures and displaying them in fun ways, you can brighten your home with the faces you love! Families who have pictures displayed around their homes give an indication that they are proud of their children and ancestors. They want to tell other people about those in the pictures.

One of my tables has photos of the women in my family from several generations. I often tell my children and grandchildren about each of their ancestors. I want them to realize where they came from. Though I display the photos in a variety of frames, it is the mother-daughter-granddaughter motif that pulls the collection together. You can group black-and-white photos, also. (The new generation likes black-and-white photos set into black frames.) Another idea is to change the pictures with the seasons. Whenever you display any collection, group items together, and remember to stage a surprise! Make sure there is one element that is a little quirky, just by being different. This feature is always a conversation-maker. Collections are just another way of sharing yourself with other people.

Prayer: Father God, as I gather together the images of my loved ones, may I be reminded to pray for these special people in my life. Amen.

Action: Take a few of those pictures which are put away and place them in frames. Add them to a new collection or to an already-existing collection.

Today's Wisdom: God sends children to enlarge our hearts, and to make us unselfish and full of kindly sympathies and affections.

—Mary Howitt

Knowing the Secret of Life

By wisdom a house is built, and through
understanding it is established;
through knowledge its rooms are filled
with rare and beautiful treasures.

—PROVERBS 24:3-4 NIV

One of our dearest friends is a classical mason. It is amazing what he does with bricks, concrete, and mortar. People wait many months just to have Jim do their brick-and stonework. He is known around town as the best, one of the last of the true craftsmen. His works will probably still be standing after 100 years.

If you would ask Jim what it takes to do a good brick fireplace, he would give you the following list:

- ✤ A proper concrete foundation

- ✤ Good bricks

- ✤ Good mortar with the right formula for sand, concrete, and water

- ✤ The correct trowels

- ✤ A good level to make sure the construction stays plumb.

Jim knows what it takes to build a good fireplace.

Often couples will ask us, "How does a couple raise good children?" We always come back to the three basic principles of today's passage:

- ～৬ wisdom
- ～৬ understanding
- ～৬ knowledge

If we raise our families with these three components, we end up with a blessing. Our rooms will be filled with "rare and beautiful treasures": Children who are respectful, obedient, polite, considerate, and who honor God.

When we are out in public places, we can readily spot the families who use these three principles. They stand out like shining stars. They reflect a radiance that the rest of society is missing.

How do we know that? Because we can see the rewards and blessings of that training. The parents have rare and beautiful treasures. Is it easy to be so blessed? No, it takes a lot of work and stick-to-it discipline to have these treasures. You have to believe that the end results can be accomplished. When you as parents have a focus, you can plan accordingly. If you have no vision, your family structure will be destroyed.

As parents and grandparents who can recognize such healthy families, do not hesitate to tell them what a great family they have. We need to shout it from the house tops: "Here is a family who has a plan for raising healthy children!"

Prayer: *Father God, give me the desire to raise healthy children. Give me the right amount of wisdom, understanding, and knowledge. Amen.*

Action: Declare together that you are going to raise a healthy family, then begin to do it.

Today's Wisdom:

Life is a flame that is always burning itself out, but it catches fire again every time a child is born.

—George Bernard Shaw

⌒

*To Christians heaven is
their everlasting home.
The most marvelous thing about it is
that God has prepared it
for those who love Him.*

—Matthew Henry

⌒

Attitude

A wise [woman] is strong, and a [woman]
of knowledge increases power.

—Proverbs 24:5

Grandchildren are so much fun. My five give me such great examples and illustrations for my writing and speaking. If I listen and watch, I can observe and hear all about life. I have one grandson, Chad, who is 20 years old now. He is either up or down—no halfway point for him. His highs are as extreme as his lows. Attitude is his saint or his demon. Over the years his biggest enemy is his attitude. For his birthday a few years ago, we gave him a coffee mug with the word *ATTITUDE* printed in bold letters. He placed it as a reminder on a shelf over his bed, so that each day upon waking, his eyes and brain would spot this cup. The printed letters were a reminder that he could choose the proper attitude for the day.

I believe that this is one of the most significant decisions that we can make on a day-to-day basis. The attitude I choose either keeps me on a positive path or hinders my progress. When my attitude is proper, nothing can stop me from accomplishing my dreams. Even when we are in a deep valley, no situation is too great for us. Our attitude is up to us.

I am glad to report that Chad no longer has to look at that mug quite as often as when he was younger. Maturity has helped him overcome a negative attitude. He has many friends, holds a key position in student government, is a member of the varsity football team, and is a member of the leadership team for his youth group at church. Chad has learned to make good choices, and his positive attitude is showing.

Prayer: *Father God, encourage me to have a good attitude each day. Let no barrier come into my life today that gives me a negative attitude. Amen.*

Action: *Choose* to have a good attitude today.

Today's Wisdom:

If you don't get everything you want, think of the things you don't get that you don't want.

—Author Unknown

☐ ☐ ☐

Adversity Versus Prosperity

If you are slack [faint] in the day of distress
[adversity], your strength is limited.

—PROVERBS 24:10

*I*f I asked you the question, "Which would you rather face: adversity or prosperity?" which would you choose? Most of us would much rather have prosperity than adversity. Prosperity gives us visions of success, money, and material things; adversity paints images of pain, suffering, and tragedy. Who in their right mind would choose suffering over plenty? And yet, adversity is a good test of our staying power and our ability to cope with difficulties, and an indicator of our ability to bounce back from defeat.

Prosperity is an even bigger test for a person than adversity. The Scottish essayist and historian Thomas Carlyle confirmed this when he said, "Adversity is sometimes hard upon a man, but for one man who can stand prosperity, there are a hundred that will stand adversity." There are many more people who have the resiliency to bounce back from difficult times than those who can handle luxury. Material blessings are harder to handle. It is hard to keep your moral, spiritual, and financial balance when you walk the tightrope of success. Just take a look at all the Hollywood stars, sports stars, and financial wizards. Star after star falls off the pinnacle of prosperity. Many of their lives are destroyed because of prosperity. In reality, most of us can handle sudden adversity much better than a large promotion.

Often the successful tend to forget about being dependent upon God. But when we are caught in the depths of adversity, there is only one thought on our mind: *survival.* During these times, family and friends come together to give us support, prayers, and words of comfort. We are flooded with uplifting Scripture passages that reassure us of our Lord's care and love.

When we hit the jackpot and are prosperous, all too often integrity seems to disappear from our character. However, those of us who are Christians realize that it is not our hands or brains that have made us successful. It is the Lord's provision. God owns everything, and we are merely stewards of His possessions.

What will adversity do to our lives? You and your family better talk about it now, for adversity hits all of us at one time or another. When cancer hit me, I never thought I would have to be concerned about that. You think it will happen to someone else, but not to you. Be grounded in the Word so you have a good spiritual understanding of how to survive when these situations of life hit you or another family member.

Prosperity requires integrity and a strong character in order for you to survive. Be ready whenever prosperity or adversity strikes your life. Both avenues require that you be prepared.

Prayer: *Father God, I thank You for my position in life. You have provided a balance of each—not too much prosperity and not too much adversity. God, You are good. Amen.*

Action: What are you going to do if either prosperity or adversity hit you? Be proactive. Do not sit back and wait. Plan now. Be prepared.

Today's Wisdom:

> There is a kind of release that comes directly to those who have undergone an ordeal and who know, having survived it, that they are equal to all of life's occasions.
>
> —Lewis Mumford

Build Your House

Prepare your work outside and
make it ready for yourself in the field;
afterwards, then, build your house.

—PROVERBS 24:27

I have heard it a million times, expressed with admiration and usually a little envy: "Oh, she's so creative."

The word *creative* often refers to an "artsy" type of person—someone who paints or writes or makes pottery. Such creative pursuits can bring great joy to those who do them and to those who enjoy the results. But you really do not have to be an artist to infuse your home and life with the spirit of creativity.

Creativity is a God-given ability to take something ordinary and make it into something special. It is an openness to doing old things in new ways and a willingness to adapt other people's good ideas to suit our personal needs. And creativity is an ability we all possess, although many of us keep it hidden in the deep corners of our lives.

Every human being is creative. The creative spirit is part of our heritage as children of the One who created all things. And nurturing our creativity is part of our responsibility as stewards of God's good gifts.

Creativity is so much more than just arts and crafts. It is a way of seeing—a willingness to see wonderful possibilities in something unformed or ordinary or even ugly.

The first year Bob and I moved to Riverside, California, we went to our first auction in an old building near Mount

Rubidoux. It was fun to see the various "treasures" that were up for sale—everything from armoires to yarn caddies—and to listen as the auctioneer shouted the bids. Then an old, greasy market scale went up, and Bob shouted an offer. I nearly died on the spot. Whatever did he think we would do with that?

He won the bid and paid 32 dollars for that ugly old scale. We went to pick it up, and I looked at it doubtfully, but Bob was sure he had bought a treasure. And he was right! He stripped the old scale clean, shined and polished it until it looked almost new, and then put it on a table. That was more than 30 years ago, and we are still enjoying Bob's imaginative purchase. It graces the narrow table behind our sofa and carries fruit in its tray, or sometimes a pot of flowers, a bowl of potpourri, or a Boston fern. Over the years, as we continue to shop for antiques, we often see scales that cost hundreds of dollars not nearly as nice as ours. I am so grateful to Bob for his creative input into our home.

One day Bob brought me another treasure from one of his antique sprees. It was a large, wooden, hand-carved rectangular bowl (another of those "What will I ever do with that thing?" items). But how I enjoy that bowl as it sits on our butcher-block island in the center of our kitchen! I keep it full of potatoes, onions, avocados, oranges, lemons, apples, and a variety of other fruits. It is not only beautiful, but very practical—another example of Bob's "creative seeing."

The kind of vision that brings the special out of the ordinary has long been part of the American tradition. Even in the tiniest frontier cabin, pioneer women found ways to express their creative urges and to add touches of loveliness to their environment.

In great-grandma's day, quilting was a wonderfully creative pursuit for women in many areas of the country. When women married or had a baby, friends and families gathered together to make the quilts the new family needed to keep warm. They used old, discarded clothing, which they cut up and patched together into colorful designs and then carefully padded and stitched to make warm coverings. The women worked, talked, and exchanged recipes. They solved garden, food, husband, and children problems—all while their hardworking fingers sewed. These quilts were truly labors of love, living testaments to the spirit of loveliness that transforms simple materials and a basic household need into a work of art and an occasion for celebration.

Our human ability to create differs from that of God in that:

ᴄᴇ He created the world out of nothing.

ᴄᴇ His creativity is unlimited (Genesis 1:1–2:3).

We are limited to doing what is in our existing natural world. Our creativity has to be expressed by thought and experience. Our manifestations are shown in our creative forms of music, art, literature, language, or problem-solving; in creating a new idea, adapting a recipe, or stretching a monthly budget. There are many ways for us humans to express ourselves with our creativity.

We tend to think we need to be original in order to be creative. But I am continually getting ideas from magazines, decorator shops, programs on the Discovery channel, by interviewing friends, and just by keeping my eyes open to life. I must be willing to make changes in the way things have always been done. I cannot be satisfied with the status quo.

The advertisers of the twenty-first century tell us we must be willing to step out of the box. This simply means to go beyond our normal experience and to be willing to expand our thoughts from the known to the unknown.

I have found that creative people are focused, committed, and disciplined in their lives. In short, they have a plan for their lives. They know where they want to go, and most of them take control of their lives and live them out God's way.

Each of us is to look inward to see what gifts God has given us. The Scriptures teach us to realize that we have divinely appointed abilities.

Do not be afraid of failure, because failure is often a stepping-stone to future successes. Failure can give us new direction in solving a particular problem.

Our home can be a wonderful laboratory in which to express our God-given talent. We can be creative in many ways:

- landscaping
- cooking
- decorating
- operating a home business
- parenting
- growing a great marriage
- designing and sewing clothes
- doing arts and crafts
- painting
- composing
- writing

One of the most valuable ways we can share the spirit of creativity is by modeling it for our children. We give them a legacy of joy when we teach them to use their God-given creativity to instill the spirit of loveliness into their own lives and homes.

Exercising our creativity is one way for us to be responsible stewards of the gifts and talents God has given us, and to rejoice in our identity as God's children, made in His image. As images of the Creator, we have the opportunity to fashion our lives and our homes into works of art. We can choose to be creative today and every day![20]

Prayer:

Father God, thank You for giving me my talents and for letting me have a spirit of loveliness. I cannot paint, sing, draw, do sculpture, design, or play an instrument, but I can dare to experiment with other talents. As such, people look at me and think I am creative. So if my friends mirror back to me that I am creative, I must be. Thanks for giving me friends who help me put my best foot forward. My desire is to encourage other women to step out and dare to be creative. Amen.

Action:

Use your imagination in displaying your collection of cups and saucers, bells, dolls, thimbles, or salt-and-pepper shakers. A side table, shelf, or armoire can serve beautifully, but so might a printer's tray, a special basket, or a windowsill. One friend of mine displayed her collection of teddy bears in a clean, but nonfunctioning fireplace.

Today's Wisdom:

God scatters beauty as he scatters flowers,
O'er the wide earth, all tells us all are ours.
A hundred lights in every temple burn,
And at each shrine I bend my knee in turn.

—Walter Savage Landor

□ □ ▢

Send Me a North Wind

The north wind brings forth rain.

—Proverbs 25:23

One of my favorite episodes of *Little House on the Prairie* concerned a mother in a small prairie town telling a story of a different time and a different place, when the wind had blown in illness and fear. "Lord, send me a north wind," she had prayed. The fresh north wind would drive away the east wind, which was sucking the breath from her father, her younger brother (six years old), and their mother when she was a young child. They were all in bed with pneumonia. There were no miracle drugs in those days, and pneumonia was all too often fatal. All rural telephone lines had snapped from the force of the driving wind. Few people would have visited their home, fearing they, too, would catch this deadly illness.

The harsh wind that threatened to bring death to this young girl's home had already taken many lives in past winters. This young girl's dear mother was out of touch with the world, but she was in touch with God. "I heard her say, 'I cannot come down with this, Lord. Send the north wind!' Our old country doctor had arrived in his horse-drawn buggy and declared, 'The crisis will come for each of them tonight; I'll stay and you pray.'"

All night the young girl and the doctor heated bricks, wrapped them in newspaper, and placed them around the sick patients. They laid cold compresses to their foreheads when they went into soaking sweats. All night long they attended one patient and then another—anything to relieve the effects of pneumonia, just to get them through the night.

The mother telling the story said that that night she had felt a weight on her chest, picked it up, and threw it through the bedroom window. To her amazement, the weight was a full hot water bottle. She recalled that immediately the room was filled with the soothing breeze which promised life to all three in her family. Soon all three who had been taken by pneumonia were awake, and her mother had shouted, "Hallelujah for the north wind."

What a great illustration this story is about our own lives. When things seem dim and there is little hope left inside our aching hearts, we can pray and ask God to send the north wind.

Prayer: *Father God, thank You for the north wind. Let me learn to patiently wait for this wind to appear in my life when all seems so helpless. Amen.*

Action: Keep in touch with God! The course of the wind will change.

Today's Wisdom:

Faith and obedience are bound up in the same bundle. He that obeys God, trusts God; and he that trusts God, obeys God.

—Charles H. Spurgeon

Watch Your Words

A lying tongue hates those it crushes,
and a flattering mouth works ruin.

—Proverbs 26:28

Those whose mouths are characterized by lies and flattery hate the victims they bring to ruin. We have to be so attentive to the words we use and to the words that are spoken by those around us. In Exodus 4:12 we read, "Now then go, and I, even I, will be with your mouth, and teach you what you are to say."

Because of the turmoil in my house as a child, I decided I would not speak, in fear that I would say the wrong thing. I became quiet and would grasp my mother's leg in order to hide from people. I did not want to be around people (particularly strangers); I was even afraid of my own family members.

My father had a major drinking problem that put everyone on pins and needles. Everyone watched what they would say around him, because Daddy would get mad very easily and make life miserable to the messenger who said the wrong thing or in the wrong way. Daddy had a lot of anger and did not like too many people.

I was this way until I got into high school and found myself being liked by my fellow classmates. As a junior, I had the female lead in our senior play, *Best Foot Forward*. My success in this performance began to instill into me some self-confidence.

It was also at this time that I met my Bob, who made me feel safe around him and his warm, friendly family. I was very quiet and reserved, for fear that I might say the wrong thing. Bob would always say, "Emilie, speak up. You've got to tell me your thoughts on this," but I was very hesitant to express myself, fearing I would say the wrong thing.

It was not until I was in my late twenties, when I signed up for a Christian women's retreat in Palm Springs, California, that I realized God had a speaking ministry for my life. Since the women of my church knew that I came from the Jewish faith, they asked me if I would give a three-minute testimony at the retreat. I felt like Moses in Exodus 4:10: "Please, Lord, I have never been eloquent, neither recently nor in time past, nor since You have spoken to Your servant; for I am slow of speech and slow of tongue." Then the Lord said to me as to Moses, "Who do you think made your mouth? Is it not I, the Lord?"

So I reluctantly said, "Yes, I'll do it." I was not sure what I would say or how I would say it, but I had confidence that my Lord and God would be on my side.

God said to Moses, "Now then go, and I, even I, will be with your mouth, and teach you what you are to say." That was a long time ago, and He still goes before me, giving me the words to say.

I can honestly say that God will be with you as you speak. I travel all over this country, sharing with women of all denominations the words He has given me to say. Along with the spoken word, He has entrusted me with writing more than 60 books, with over four million copies in print.

My testimony was so well-received by those in the audience that I received many invitations to go to local women's clubs to share my story.

Am I still nervous when I get up to speak? Yes, every time. I still have to rely upon God each time I speak to give me a peace and calm before I begin. I often ask, "Why me, Lord? There are many better speakers and writers than I am." But God always answers back, "Now then go, and I will be with your mouth and teach you what to say."

So watch your words. Choose to use those that reflect love, rather than those which divide and hurt.

Prayer: *Father God, I am amazed that You have been able to use me—an ordinary wife, mother, and grandmother. You take the ordinary and make it extraordinary. May I always be willing to share my story as long as there are those who want to hear it. I lay my "bouquet of flowers" at the foot of the cross each night. Amen.*

Action: Do not hold back saying yes to God because of fear.

Today's Wisdom:

       I shall be telling this with a sigh somewhere ages and ages hence; two roads diverged in a wood, and I, I took the one less traveled by—and that has made all the difference.

                            —Robert Frost

Enough's Enough

He who is full loathes honey,
but to the hungry even what is bitter tastes sweet.

—PROVERBS 27:7 NIV

Our materialistic society tells us we must acquire more, bigger, and better. We not only have to keep up with the Joneses, but we also must have all that our TVs and full-page colored ads tell us we must have in order to be cool. Highly educated and sophisticated adults respond with teenage jargon: "Cool." If it is not cool to the masses, we do not want to wear it, drive in it, fly in it, or eat at it.

The Scriptures encourage us to be content in whatever circumstance we find ourselves (Philippians 4:11). In our "have-it-all" society, this definition goes against the grain. Society says we can only be content when we have. How can we balance the things we need with the things we want? One of our great tensions in life is to determine the difference between "need" and "want." Over the years, my husband, Bob, and I have learned to put a limit on our desires. There are a lot of things we can afford but do not buy. We find it challenging to walk away from a sales pitch. At times it becomes a game with us. People cannot understand why we do not buy something when we can afford it.

Long ago, we decided together (very important) that this is where we stop. We do not need any bigger or better trophies to make us happy. It has not always been easy to sort out where to draw the line in the sand, especially when there are so many wonderful and inviting things to do and places to go, but God has always rewarded our efforts to simplify.

When we as a family put a ceiling on our desires, we are saying to the people around us, "We can be happy in the present." It means that we are training ourselves to live out the adage that "More is not always better."

Placing a ceiling on our desires is also a great way to eliminate stress. I can guarantee you, contentment will give you great joy. Make this a matter of prayer and discussion with your family. It is one of the most valuable concepts that you can pass along to your children.

Prayer: *Father God, I want You and whatever You choose to provide. Give me the grace to let the rest go and to trust You for my real needs. Amen.*

Action: Draw a line in the sand between what you want versus what you need. Discuss with your mate what you envision as a ceiling on your desires.

Today's Wisdom:

To have what we want is riches, but to be able to do without is power.

—Donald Grant

Little Eyes Are Watching

As iron sharpens iron, so one [woman]
sharpens another....As water reflects a face,
so a [woman's] heart reflects the [woman].

—PROVERBS 27:17,19 NIV

I often hear mothers comment that over and over
they tell their children this and that, but in a day or two they
have to tell their children the same things again. "Don't they
ever learn?" they ask. Even if a mother raises her voice an
octave, it does not make any difference on her children's
behavior. What does a parent have to do to get their attention?

First of all, what kind of an example are you? We think
it is our words that matter with other people, but when it
comes to influencing those around us, our actions often
speak louder than our words.

We teach by example in our homes, at the beach, while
jogging, while praying, while resting, while eating—in every
part of the day. You will find that children will imitate the
values we exhibit in our home and about them. Little eyes
are peering out to see how we behave when no one is
looking. Simple things are noticed, like lighted candles on
a table or the thank-you you offer when food is being served
in a restaurant—even how you respond when a policeman
writes you a ticket. How is your demeanor? Are your actions
consistent with what you say you believe?

If you believe it is important to be patient, then how do you respond when you are standing in line at the supermarket? If you believe it is important to be a good neighbor, then do you send a quick thank-you note (not an e-mail) for a gift or thoughtful kindness?

We are continually setting some kind of example (positive or negative), whether we know it or not. It is as simple as that! Make sure your speech matches your actions. If it does not, you will not be teaching values that will be grasped by onlookers.

Prayer: *Father God, thank You for those people who influence me, and I pray that I might become a person whose influence draws others toward You. Amen.*

Action: Examine how well your actions follow your speech. What needs improvement?

Today's Wisdom:

A person should always remember that the value of his good works is not based on their number and excellence, but on the love of God which prompts the person to do these things.

—Juan de la Cruz

Leaving a Legacy

*Know well the condition of your flocks, and pay
attention to your herds; for riches are not forever,
nor does a crown endure to all generations.*

—PROVERBS 27:23-24

What kind of legacy are you going to leave to your heirs? According to Webster's Dictionary, the word *legacy* means:

- Money or property left to someone by a will bequest

- Anything handed down from, or as from, an ancestor

It is exciting to realize that you will leave something behind, even if it is only in the way people remember you. Sometimes it can be a memory, a tradition, a character value learned, a smile, an apple pie. Other times it can be in a material form of objects and things.

In 2 Timothy 1:5 we see a legacy in action when Paul says, "I am mindful of the sincere faith within you, which first dwelt in your grandmother Lois, and your mother Eunice, and I am sure that it is in you as well." It is easy to think of a legacy in terms of financial resources or material possessions. But have you ever considered the value of leaving behind the qualities of faith, hope, and love to those who love and cherish you?

You and I have the incredible opportunity to leave behind a legacy—one of care and concern, one that reaches out to other people, one of loveliness and holiness. Be a mom who cares about what kind of legacy you leave when the Lord calls you home. Follow God's plan for you—just you! Pattern your life from what you have learned through the Scriptures. Be a woman of character and principles. Simply pass the legacy on to those who will follow.

Prayer: *Father God, may those who follow me have a fond remembrance of who I was in Christ. My prayer is that each one of my grandchildren will know and claim You as his or her Savior. There is no greater legacy than this. Amen.*

Action: Polish up a crisp apple and enjoy it with your favorite cheese.

Today's Wisdom:
It is important that a wise person passes on wisdom—not only in words, but in deeds. Little eyes are looking to see if you are authentic.

Oftentimes Less Is Best

A faithful [woman] will abound with blessings.

—Proverbs 28:20

ave you ever met people with limited income who are rich, and rich people who are poor? I certainly have, and I love to see how different people stretch their money to become wealthy. I have a very good friend who can make a purse out of a sow's ear. She knows how to shop. She lives in a very affluent area of Southern California, so she takes great delight in going into second-time-around stores to purchase very nice clothing at greatly reduced prices. Another friend has made her rental condo into a dollhouse. She takes old furniture and gives it the latest artistic touch, and she adds a few touches with fabric accents that she makes on her sewing machine. My Bob used to have a barber whose wife loved to drive a Lincoln Town Car, but they could not afford one on his income. They would watch the ads and rent one for the weekend. That was just enough to satisfy her need for wanting to drive a large car.

Another couple I know love to camp along the California coastline. For very little cost they visit a different state park each year and have a wonderful time with their family. They—and you—can find happiness within a budget.

Do not spend time thinking about what you do not have, but count your blessings in the things you do have. Do not wait until the next big raise to do something bigger than you are used to. Instead, find happiness where you are. Make the best and most of what you have. One way to minimize the stress over a tight budget is to make the decision to stop using a lack of funds to justify your unhappiness. This is not an "if only I had" world. Enjoy what you have as much as possible.[21]

Prayer: *Father God, my life has been full of wonderful blessings from You. You have generously given to me out of Your abundance. Every day I am thankful for everything You bless me with. Amen.*

Action: Do something fun this weekend that costs little or no money.

Today's Wisdom:

Right now the people in the United States owe over one trillion dollars on their credit cards. The number goes higher every year.

That means the borrowers are paying 150 billion dollars every year in interest—a staggering amount.

—Source Unknown

A Friendship Tea

*The heartfelt counsel of a friend
is as sweet as perfume.*

—Proverbs 27:9 nlt

*P*eople are longing for friendship. We are a country of people who are becoming friendless. Our high technology lets us close ourselves off from the outside world. We isolate ourselves so that we do not have to communicate with someone else. Even in restaurants we see young children sitting with their families and not talking. Why? They have some electronic game in their hands. We have become islands unto ourselves. One way to break this trend is to have a seasonal tea party, with no electronic devices allowed. Parties with friends (also invite some people who are new to the gathering) offer a lot of opportunity to converse.

An afternoon tea is a great way to celebrate friendship. What would you do without those chosen sisters who laugh with you, cry with you, and speak truth to you? What better way to celebrate your friendship than with the intimacy of a friendship tea?

Select the kind of food you like best. Order it, or choose a menu you can prepare a day ahead. That way you are relaxed and getting into the spirit of a soothing tea before your friends arrive. You can greet each guest with a calm manner, instead of the intensity that comes from last-minute rushing. Music from a CD player in the background works great. A friend recently had a tea in the garden of her home

243

to celebrate her own successful gardening efforts. Her favorite friends were invited for the celebration of her efforts. A tea is as much about friendship as it is about tea. Get those invitations ready, and let your friends know how special they are in your life.

Truly, a dear friend who can stick beside you in good times as well as difficult times is as a sweet perfume. She gives you comfort and support when you need it. Her fragrance sweetens the air around you. Cherish your friends, for they are one of your most valuable assets.

Prayer: *Father God, where two or more are gathered in Your name, You are there. I feel Your presence when I am among my closest friends. How grateful I am for being surrounded by love. Amen.*

Action: Plan to have a friendship tea within the next six weeks. Send your invitations out early.

Today's Wisdom:

Friends are necessary to a happy life. When friendship deserts us we are as lonely and helpless as a ship, left by the tide high upon the shore. When friendship returns to us, it is as though the tide came back, gave us buoyancy and freedom, and opened to us the wide places of the world.

—Harry Emerson Fosdick

Be Content

Give me neither poverty nor riches.

—Proverbs 30:8

often have heard it said, "I have been rich and I have been poor, and I like rich better." Of course we do! However, being rich has its own unique responsibilities. Paul writes in Philippians 4:11-12, "I have learned to be content in whatever circumstances I am. I know how to get along with humble means and I also know how to live in prosperity; in any and every circumstance. I have learned the secret of being filled and going hungry, both of having abundance and suffering need." Paul knew how to live beyond his external circumstances. The secret of such contentment is found in verse 13: "I can do all things through Him who strengthens me."

One of our Barnes family mottos is, "You will not be content with what you want, if you are not content with what you have." Do not waste your whole life waiting for your boat to come in. I have a good friend who often worries that when her boat comes in she will be at the train station.

Praise God every day for what He has so graciously given you. We are to be good stewards of all things from God, either in little or in much.

Some people sit around waiting to win the lottery or the Clearing House sweepstakes. But winning it might not be good for some of us. Sudden wealth could hurt us spiritually.

Agur, the writer of Proverbs 30, did not ask God for wealth. He was afraid that if he were rich he might feel self-sufficient and try to live without God. Some of us cannot be trusted with wealth. So do not necessarily set your heart on it. Instead, thank God for what you have and be content. Then use whatever God has trusted you with for His glory. God wants us to be generous with whatever we have. After all, riches are relative. At whatever level you are, be content and say, "Thank You." If you have been blessed with wealth, it is a double blessing: first, for you, and second, for the blessing of other people who are not as fortunate.

Prayer: *Father God, I truly want to be a content person. Let my heart cry out, "Thank You, God, for all You have given me. I know that riches and honor come from You." Amen.*

Action: Tell God how thankful you are for all He has given you.

Today's Wisdom:
Make all you can, save all you can, give all you can.

—John Wesley

Smell the Roses

*The way of an eagle in the sky, the way of a serpent
on a rock, the way of a ship in the middle of the sea,
and the way of a man with a maid.*

—PROVERBS 30:19

The writer of Proverbs says that four things are wonderful, and he does not comprehend them:

- the way of an eagle in the sky
- the way of a serpent on a rock
- the way of a ship in the middle of the sea
- the way of a man with a maid

Each one of these four wonders means that you have to stop what you are doing and observe what is going on around you. All of us have to stop and take time to smell the roses. Get off that merry-go-round and learn to see and appreciate what is going on in God's creation.

Life is full of simple pleasures that bring calm to our spirits and delight to our senses. Here are some reminders of the simple pleasures of life:

- the sun on the back of your neck
- the smell of bacon or coffee first thing in the morning
- chocolate-chip cookies when you come in the door in the afternoon

❧ singing in church

❧ making a new friend

❧ finding money in the couch

❧ getting into a freshly made bed

❧ making someone smile

❧ getting a tax refund

❧ getting a new hairstyle

❧ moonlight on the ocean

❧ the smell of freshly mowed grass

❧ having exact change at the toll booth

❧ fishing with Dad

❧ new slippers

❧ watching your children when they are sleeping

❧ the sound of rain on the roof

❧ licking the frosting bowl

❧ wearing a new dress

❧ browsing in a bookstore

❧ two scoops of ice cream

❧ being excited about today

Psalm 116:6 states, "The LORD preserves the simple." Do not miss the abundance of simple pleasures in your everyday activities.

Prayer: *Father God, I bask in Your goodness. I wonder at the world You have created for me to live in. You are a great God. I am looking forward to smelling the roses today. Amen.*

Action:　　Keep your life simple.

Today's Wisdom:

A garden is a place where little miracles occur every moment.

—Sue Muszala

In the town of Woeden in Germany,
on the tower of a fine church building
is the carved figure of a lamb.
It was placed there to
commemorate the remarkable escape
from death of a workman who fell
from the high scaffolding when
the tower was being built.
At the moment of his fall a flock of
sheep was being driven by,
and he had fallen on one of the lambs,
which was crushed to death.
The carved figure of the lamb
was placed there to commemorate the incident,
and also to remind all
who came that way of the Lamb
of God who died to save sinners.

—A. NAISMITH

Find Peace and Rest

The ants are not a strong people,
but they prepare their food in the summer.

—Proverbs 30:25

ave you ever taken the time to study ants? For their size, their feats are unbelievable. If ants were humans, they would own all the world records in any sport. When Bob was a teacher, he would have his sixth-grade students build an "ant farm." Every year this was one of his favorite science projects. The students were amazed at these little folks. As soon as the students entered the class, they would go over to the glass box and see what these little giants had done overnight. New mounds were formed, new tunnels dug, and new ants multiplied. They were busy, busy, busy.

I get exhausted just watching some people who are as busy as ants. Life can be overwhelming. Please slow down. As women, let's make it our goal to keep life simple.

My Bob and I were returning home one afternoon from doing errands, and our route took us over a large bridge. Bob started telling me how the workers on this bridge never finish their work. That sounded familiar! He went on to tell me that as soon as the maintenance personnel finish chipping away the rust and painting their engineering marvel, they have to start all over again. They go back to the beginning and do it all over. Their work is never done. Not even the color gets to change.

As homemakers, we are faced with the same problem. When it comes to taking care of our homes, there is always something needing repair, replacement, repainting, renovating, or something! Our job never seems to end. I had a lady call me on the phone one day crying because about the time she got organized, everything got messed up again. I assured her that this is life. As long as we live with other people, things will get out of place, and you have to organize all over again. For some reason, she thought that once you got organized, you stayed organized for life. That just is not reality. It would be great if it worked like that, but realistically it does not.

Grasp the truth that life is a process and our homes are in process. God intended us to live and grow, and growth is a process. Hang in there, keep it simple, and be flexible. As you do the dishes for the third time today, be grateful that you have dishes to wash and food to dirty them. A lot of people in this world would love to have our problems.

Prayer: *Father God, today I feel overwhelmed. Please calm my heart and my mind. Bring stillness to my troubled waters. I will rest in Your peace today. Amen.*

Action: Put on jogging shoes and clean house to some fast-paced music.

Today's Wisdom:

Lord, thou madest us for thy self, and we can find no rest till we find rest in thee.

—St. Augustine

☐ ☐ ☐

What Do Women Do All Day?

A wife of noble character who can find? She is
worth far more than rubies. Her husband has full
confidence in her and lacks nothing of value.

—Proverbs 31:10-11

Have you ever had your husband ask you, "What do you women do all day?" That is one of the mystery questions of life. The answer to this question depends upon two roles which you might have: one, that of a full-time homemaker, and two, that of a homemaker plus having a full-time job outside the home. The alternative question your husband asks might be, "How was work today?" It is just a friendly question, where he wants to be caught up on you and your outside job. But if it is a question asked when you are "only" a full-time homemaker, the question might be asked for a different reason.

Many times a husband does not understand what his wife does. I often challenge women to plan a time when Dad has to take care of the home for an occasional weekend, just to experience what women do around the home. He will be so excited to see you come back home. This will give him a positive appreciation for your role as a homemaker. He will finally see the light.

Several years ago, Marshall H. Hart wrote in *Home Life* magazine:

> Every minute, to and fro, that's the way my hours go;
> Bring me this, and take me that, feed the dog, and take out the cat.
>
> Standing up, I eat my toast, drink my coffee, thaw the roast,
> Empty garbage, make the bed, rush to church, then wash my head.
>
> Sweep the kitchen, wash the floor, scrub the woodwork, clean the doors;
> Scour the bathtub, then myself. Vacuum carpets, straighten shelves.
>
> Eat my sandwich on the run...now my afternoon's begun.
> To the baseball game I go, when will there be time to sew?
>
> Meet the teacher, stop the fight, see the dentist, fly the kite.
> Help with homework, do the wash, iron the clothes, put on the squash.
>
> Shop for groceries, cash a check, fight the crowds, now I'm a wreck!
> Dinner time it soon will be. "What's for supper?" Wait and see!
>
> Dirty dishes crowd the sink, next there's popcorn, then a drink.
> Will they never go to bed? Will I ever get ahead?
>
> "Bring me water," "Get the light." Turn off TV, lock the bike."
> "Where's my pillow?" "Hear my prayers." "Did you lock the door downstairs?"
>
> At last in bed, my spouse and I, too tired to move, too weak to cry.
> But e'er I doze, I hear him say, "WHAT DO WOMEN DO ALL DAY?"[22]

Yes, mothers, we know what women do all day. You might need to establish a public-relations campaign which lets your observing family know what you do. One way is to delegate jobs to other members of your family, such as setting the table, washing the dishes, keeping their rooms picked up, assisting in housecleaning, ironing their own clothes, helping in meal planning, running errands for you. This way they begin to get an appreciation for the role you play in the family. This also helps train your children for adulthood. After all, Mom will not always be around to do everything for them as they branch out on their own.

Prayer: *Father God, I thank You for making me a woman. I love how You created me. I feel that I have the most creative and demanding job on earth. I would not trade it for any other profession. May I exhibit good stewardship in my position. Amen.*

Action: Treat yourself to a special day away from your routine. Invite a friend to go out to lunch, to a movie, for tea, to get a massage, to spend a few hours at the spa, etc. Treat yourself specially for one day.

Today's Wisdom:

     We have been called to serve as a mother, a woman, and a wife. We are to serve not only with our hands, but also with our hearts.

Know Your Man

*She gets up while it is still dark; she provides food
for her family and portions for her servant girls.*

—PROVERBS 31:15

We have often heard the saying about the power of a chocolate-chip cookie to win a young man's heart. Such a suitor rejoices the day when this lovely young maiden brings him a platter of chocolate-chip cookies fresh from the oven. In his mind he hears his heart cry out, "Utopia! I have finally found the love of my life. I know this is the one God has sent to me."

Your mother may have told you a century-old truth about men: "The way to a man's heart is through his stomach." These two trite sayings seem so simple, when in reality they carry a lot of truth.

There is power in chocolate-chip cookies. There is power in finding out what pleases a man. I know from experience, and I know from the mail I receive, specifically letters from husbands whose wives make great improvements in their homemaking and organizational skills after attending one of our seminars. What happens in three hours that changes a wife so dramatically? The secret is not a little pill or a magic word. Instead, I offer a biblical perspective on being a wife and homemaker, holding out the hope that women can indeed change the way their home is functioning. I share ideas about how to lighten their load and even make homemaking fun. One reason why this kind of message is important is because men need to know that their wives can handle the household and children in an organized and efficient way. The stereotypical male fantasy of coming home to a well-cooked meal, cooperative and well-behaved children, and a kiss at the door is not too far off from what men really do want!

Why is an organized, smoothly functioning home important to a man? Because he needs a place to unwind after a day at work. When Bob arrived home, he used to always say to me, "You think I'm home, but I just sent my body ahead of me!" In reality, he would not be home for another 30 minutes. During that half hour he regrouped. He did not handle any emergencies or deal with any bad news. I would often get him a cold drink and let him sit in his favorite chair, where he could even take a brief nap. That time allowed him to change gears. After 30 minutes, he was truly home and able to function as a member of the family.

Bob was able to unwind because our home was well-organized and functioning smoothly. If I had not taken the time over the years to put some good practices into our home, we would have fallen victim to disorganization, too.

As our Scripture verse teaches today, the woman of the home has some very challenging roles. The woman who comments, "The homemaker role is not stimulating enough for me. I have to get a job outside of the home to find purpose," has never considered the Proverbs 31 woman as a role model. There is a whole lifetime to implement these tasks, so roll up your sleeves and begin today.[23]

Prayer: *Father God, thank You for reminding me that it is the little things that count in life. Let me dwell on this truth today. I sometimes get so caught up in the big things that I forget the preciousness of simplicity. Amen.*

Action: Make your loved ones a batch of chocolate-chip cookies.

Today's Wisdom:

Oatmeal Chocolate-Chip Cookie Recipe

Ingredients:
¾ C. brown sugar
¾ C. butter
¾ C. white sugar
2 eggs, beaten
2 Tbsp. hot water
2 C. flour
1 tsp. soda
1 tsp. salt
1 pkg. chocolate chips
1½–2 C. oatmeal
1 C. nuts (optional)
1 Tbsp. vanilla

Directions: Blend first six ingredients together in a mixing bowl. Mix the remaining ingredients together and blend with the first six. After blending the two mixes together, put spoonfuls of cookie dough on a flat, ungreased cookie sheet. Bake at 350° for approximately 7 minutes. Cool cookies on a cookie rack.

—Source: *Words into Type,*
3rd ed. p. 112

□ □ □

To Be a Mom

She extends her hands to the poor,
and she stretches out her hands to the needy.

—Proverbs 31:20

When God made a mom, He made a very unique person. Only God could have put together such components in one body. I am certainly glad that we are different from a man (not that God did not do a good job in His creation, but I like being a mom much better than I would have being a dad).

A woman has to be able to run on black coffee and leftovers. Often she runs on little sleep and always seems to be tired. She has to give kisses that can cure anything from a broken leg to a disappointing relationship. She has to have six pairs of hands and ears that can listen to, hear, and interpret every need of her family.

You are one of those moms. Just think what an important part of God's creation you are. You are the glue that holds your family together. Today we need millions of mothers who understand their role and proceed with great confidence. We need Christian moms who will stand boldly before the world and not budge. Never feel ashamed of your commitment to such a vital job. And never second-guess that your role of mother is anything less than significant and God-pleasing!

We need you very much. Do not give up on the task God has given you. The world needs godly women who will model and promote righteousness. Create for yourself a network of other moms who share your convictions, who will inspire you to be your best, and who will encourage you during the hard days.

Be sure to be an encourager to women you meet and know who are earnestly attempting to be godly women. Some days can be so discouraging and every bit of edification is appreciated.

Prayer: *Father God, thank You for making mothers unique. May women seek Your help and Your strength as they commit to forming lives and establishing a foundation of faith for their children. Amen.*

Action: Thank God for motherhood.

Today's Wisdom:

Children are the most wholesome part of the race, the sweetest, for they are freshest from the hand of God. Whimsical, ingenious, mischievous, they fill the world with joy and good humor. We adults live a life of apprehension as to what they will think of us; a life of defense against their terrifying energy; a life of hard work to live up to their great expectations. We put them to bed with a sense of relief—and greet them in the morning with delight and anticipation. We envy them the freshness of adventure and the discovery of life. In all these ways, children add to the wonder of being alive. In all these ways, they help to keep us young.

—Herbert Hoover

□ □ □

A Woman of Virtue

*Her husband is known in the gates, when he sits
among the elders of the land.*

—Proverbs 31:23

God has a calling for all women. Some are to be wives, mothers, merchants, real-estate brokers, lawyers, nurses, doctors, etc. We each have a calling. Whatever our calling might be, we are to do it to the best of our ability. Martin Luther expressed it well: "A dairyman can milk his cows unto the Lord."

Once upon a time there lived in a three-story yellow house with white trimming a little boy named Jimmy. Each evening as he came down the narrow, English-elm-lined lane, Jimmy announced the end of the school day with a whistle. The merry little notes brought his little Scotch mother to the window with a smile of welcome. His mother was a great lover of poetry, old romantic tales, and old ballads. The little boy's happiest moments were those spent listening to her various readings. He enjoyed a rich imagination—even pretending medieval characters were walking to and from school in Cambridge with him. History was in the making, with echoes of Lord Perry's artillery still rumbling along the street, but Jimmy was more interested in "boy things": bows and arrows, whale's teeth, and a cockatoo in the village barbershop, which, the barber assured him, spoke the Hottentot language. His imagination grew.

Jimmy grew up, as little boys do, and went away to school. When he graduated from Harvard, he found himself faced with the necessity of making a decision about an occupation. He felt no interest in becoming a minister like his father. He did not wish to be a doctor. There was law, which he chose from necessity, not love. His love was for poetry, but such thinking was folly, the young man was taught to believe.

Then Jimmy met Maria White, who loved the stories his mother loved, and who loved poetry as he loved it. "I want to be the wife of a poor man!" she declared. Her declaration gave us James Russell Lowell.

If you had the opportunity to visit this American poet's home, you could view the little cemetery where his first-born daughter rests. From there you could see the tiny headstone. But a more lasting monument was the sorrow-painted picture he sketched with immortal words: "The First Snowfall." Looking from his study window at the tiny grave, Lowell compared the drifting snow to patience given by the hands of the Almighty Father from clouds of snow to bless and comfort in grief. The whole literary world can rejoice that James Russell Lowell had an unselfish wife. Maria White had a calling from God. She was to be the inspiration that brought out the best in her husband—not a wealthy man, but a man who was very sensitive and gifted with the right words.

Prayer: *Father God, may I be known as a woman who is not selfish. I want to be an encourager to my husband and my family. I pray that You will give me the patience and desire to be this kind of woman. Amen.*

Action: Thank God for unselfish women.

Today's Wisdom:

But all who humble themselves before the LORD shall be given every blessing, and shall have wonderful peace.

—Psalm 37:11 TLB

Jesus loves me this I know,
For the Bible tells me so.
Little ones to Him belong—
They are weak but He is strong.

—ANNA B. WARNER

Building a Strong Family

She watches over the affairs of her household.

—Proverbs 31:27 NIV

Women often ask me how to build a strong family. There is not a simple answer to that question. Authors have written entire books attempting to offer the answer, often without arriving at a consensus.

I do know a few things about strong families, though. One is just how important they can be during unexpected adversity. During my recent serious illness, the various members of our family have been the force behind my recovery. If I did not realize it before, I realize it now: Family is so very, very important. When all is said and done, family is the most important part of a person's life. Without good families, there would not be as much joy as there is.

I have noticed a few common threads among the strong families I know, and perhaps these might offer some insight:

- All strong families have the ability to express open appreciation and affection. There are a lot of hugs, kisses, and pats on the back. The commonly spoken phrases include "I love you," "You are great," "You add a lot to our family."

- Often the mothers in these families nurture spiritual well-being. Each member seems willing to act as a stress absorber for others in the family when necessary. Strong families know they are there for each other for the duration. Family ranks very high on every family member's priority list.

❧ The strong sense of family manifests itself by a desire to engage in joint activities, rather than each person going his or her own way. Birthdays, anniversaries, holidays, and other important family dates (as well as family history) are big deals. A lot of family photographs are displayed around the home.

❧ Rewards and awards are often given for the slightest achievements. In our family, recognition was given by using our famed red "You Are Special" plate.

❧ Genuine spirituality is a family project. Issues are discussed, the Bible is read, prayers are spoken, meals are blessed, the poor remembered.

All these elements help to make healthy families. After all, "As our families go, so goes America."[24]

Prayer: *Father God, the older I get, the more important is family. I thank You for the wonderful family You have given me. They are the heart and purpose for my life. Amen.*

Action: Plan an activity that the whole family would enjoy. Include the grandparents, if they are available.

Today's Wisdom:

Parents have become so convinced that educators know what is best for their children that they forget that they themselves are really the experts.

—Marian Wright Edelman

Raise Up a Son

Her children rise up and bless her.

—Proverbs 31:28

At one time in America's history, sons grew up through boyhood and emerged from adolescence into stalwart manhood. But that is not true anymore. Our cultural clash has attempted to feminize our young men to be more soft, gentle, and not as aggressive. We all know that moderation has some redeeming values, but we have gone overboard. One of the challenges of the twenty-first century is to develop men in the fashion that God intended.

Mom and Dad have to be very focused in how they are going to accomplish this task. The subject warrants an entire book, but we want to challenge you this day to realize that raising a son is not as easy as it used to be. As parents and grandparents, we have some forces to contend with that have never been as compelling as they are today.

General Douglas MacArthur, that great general in World War II, had a special prayer for his son. It may have particular meaning for you, Mom and Dad, in raising your son(s):

> Build me a son, O Lord, who will be strong enough to know when he is weak, and brave enough to face himself when he is afraid; one who will be proud and unbending in honest defeat, and humble and gentle in victory.
>
> Build me a son whose wishbone will not be where his backbone should be; a son who will know thee and that to know himself is the foundation stone of knowledge.

266 —の Emilie Barnes

Lead him, I pray, not in the path of ease and comfort, but under the stress and spur of difficulties and challenge. Here let him learn to stand up in the storm; here let him learn compassion for those who fail.

Build me a son whose heart will be clear, whose goal will be high; a son who will master himself before he seeks to master other men; one who will learn to laugh, yet never forget how to weep; one who will reach into the future, yet never forget the past.

And after all these things are his, add, I pray, enough of a sense of humor, so that he may always be serious, yet never take himself too seriously. Give him humility, so that he may always remember the simplicity of true greatness, the open mind of true wisdom, the meekness of true strength.

Then I, his father, will dare to whisper, "I have not lived in vain."[24]

Prayer: *Father God, may You give us a heart for raising our sons to become men of God. We sometimes feel so inadequate for this adventure. Boys seem so rough and tough. We do want to be stretched in this assignment so that we can also say, "I have not lived in vain." Amen.*

Action: Let your sons be responsible for their own actions. Resist solving their problems.

Today's Wisdom:

A boy is Truth with dirt on his face, Beauty with a cut on his finger, Wisdom with bubble gum in his hair, and the Hope of the future with a frog in his pocket.

—Alan Beck

Work unto the Lord

*Give her the product of her hands, and let her
works praise her in the gates.*

—Proverbs 31:31

For some reason we think that the trend of women going to work started during World War II, when women had to fill the gap while the men were away defending our country. But today's Scripture reading goes back to about 800 B.C. Long before we even thought of women being in the labor force, this capable woman was an energetic, hard worker, who labored far into the night. She was a woman with many virtues (read Proverbs 31:10-31).

This woman knew all about work, even though she did not have an MBA from Harvard or Stanford. She was a woman who feared (respected) God, and because of her noble efforts in the workplace, she was praised.

In today's work climate, we find that Monday is the most difficult day of the week, with the most absenteeism, the most accidents, the most illnesses. Many of today's workers focus on Fridays—the getaway days. In fact, a popular restaurant is named TGI Friday (Thank God It's Friday). If you go into this restaurant to eat, you sense a party atmosphere. It is a place to forget all your cares. Let's have a party!

This attitude has a lot to say about modern man and woman's approach to work. It is a far cry from the day when the adage was, "To pray is to work, to work is to pray." In those days, work was a reflection of worship to God. When

267

we worked, we worked to the Lord, not for the pleasing of man. That is when the artisan was a creator of excellence in art, music, literature, and the professions. It is our own attitude toward work that reflects the joy of the Lord.

Oh, if we could recapture this concept of work! We would take the drudgeries of everyday life and give them to God. If we took the routines surrounding our work and began to pray about them, I believe our whole attitude would change for ourselves and those in our family. No longer would we wait for the whistle to blow on Friday so we could let real life begin. For us every day would be a Friday.

In Genesis we read that in the beginning God *created.* He believed in the honor of work. It was a godly activity. It was not cursed, as it is today. God worked for six days and then rested. How is your rest period? Do you get any?

Jesus, a carpenter, was a worker making goods out of wood. The Scriptures teach that if we are not willing to work, we should not expect to eat.

How do we learn that to pray is to work, and to work is to pray?

- ❧ Each morning when we wake up, we thank God for a new day and all that is in it.

- ❧ We offer to God in worship all of our energies, creativity, time, and skills.

- ❧ We recognize that work done in an attitude of prayer brings excellence, which in turn bears testimony to God.

- ❧ We realize that we are obedient to God when we provide for our family and their needs.

- ❧ We model to our children that work is good, so that they see us give worship to God for the work He has given us.[26]

Prayer: Father God, at times when I face drudgery in all that I have to do, when I wipe the sweat from my brow and my back aches from the weight of lifting, I forget that how I do my job is a reflection upon my worship to You. I truly want to wake up each morning with a song in my heart and an eagerness to start a new day. In the evening before I fall asleep, I want to praise You for another day's work. Let me be in continuous prayer while at work. Let me work for You and forget about the praises of man. Amen.

Action: Thank God for the skills He has given you to perform worship to Him.

Today's Wisdom:

It is our best work that He wants, not the dregs of our exhaustion. I think He must prefer quality to quantity.

—George MacDonald

Notes

1. Emilie Barnes, *15 Minutes Alone with God* (Eugene, OR: Harvest House Publishers, 1994), pp. 69-70.

2. Emilie Barnes, *15 Minutes Alone with God*, pp. 69-70.

3. Emilie Barnes, *Minute Meditations for Healing and Hope* (Eugene, OR: Harvest House Publishers, 2003), adapted from pp. 57-58.

4. Bob Barnes, *Minute Meditations for Men* (Eugene, OR: Harvest House Publishers, 1998), pp. 269-70.

5. June Masters Bacher, *Quiet Moments for Women* (Eugene, OR: Harvest House Publishers, 1979), February 24.

6. Unknown source.

7. Emilie Barnes, *15 Minutes Alone with God*, pp. 223-26.

8. Emilie Barnes, *15 Minute of Peace with God* (Eugene, OR: Harvest House Publishers, 1997), pp. 52-55.

9. Bob and Emilie Barnes, *Minute Meditations for Busy Moms* (Eugene, OR: Harvest House Publishers, 2003), adapted from pp. 141-42.

10. Emilie Barnes, *15 Minutes of Peace with God*, adapted from pp. 237-39.

11. Emilie Barnes, *15 Minutes Alone with God*, pp. 107-08.

12. Emilie Barnes, *Minute Meditations for Women* (Eugene, OR: Harvest House Publishers, 1999), pp. 211-12.

13. Emilie Barnes, *Minute Meditations for Busy Women* (Eugene, OR: Harvest House Publishers, 2003), pp. 145-46.

14. Emilie Barnes, *15 Minutes of Peace with God*, pp. 146-51.

15. Emilie Barnes, *Minute Meditations for Women*, pp. 85-86.

16. Charles R. Swindoll, *You and Your Child* (Nashville, TN: Thomas Nelson Publishers, 1977), p. 64.

17. Emilie Barnes, *15 Minutes of Peace with God*, adapted from pp. 220-23.

18. Steve Farrar, *Standing Tall* (Sister, OR: Multnomah Books, 1994), pp. 51-52.

19. Emilie Barnes, *Minute Meditations for Couples* (Eugene, OR: Harvest House Publishers, 2001), pp. 265-66.

20. Emilie Barnes, *15 Minutes of Peace with God*, adapted from pp. 227-31.

21. Emilie Barnes, *Minute Meditations for Women*, pp. 29-30.

22. Marshall H. Hart, *Home Life* magazine (date unknown).

23. Emilie Barnes, *15 Minutes Alone with God*, adapted from pp. 235-37.

24. Emilie Barnes, *Minute Meditations for Busy Moms*, pp. 192-93.

25. Brian Culhane, comp., *The Treasure Chest* (New York: Harper Collins Publishers, 1995), p. 91.

26. Emilie Barnes, *15 Minutes of Peace with God*, adapted from pp. 60-63.

Other Harvest House Books
by Emilie Barnes

ও ও ও

The 15-Minute Organizer

15 Minutes Alone with God

*15 Minutes of Peace
with God*

101 Ways to Lift Your Spirits

*101 Ways to Love Your
Grandkids*

Cleaning Up the Clutter

*Emilie's Creative Home
Organizer*

*Everything I Know
I Learned from My Garden*

Home Warming

*A Grandma Is a Gift
From God*

If Teacups Could Talk

I Need Your Strength, Lord

An Invitation to Tea

Join Me for Tea

*Keep It Simple
for Busy Women*

Let's Have a Tea Party!

A Little Book of Manners

*Minute Meditations
for Busy Moms*

*Minute Meditations for
Healing and Hope*

*Minute Meditations
for Women*

*Minute Meditations on
Prayer*

More Faith in My Day

More Hours in My Day

*Quiet Moments for a Busy
Mom's Soul*

A Quiet Refuge

Safe in the Father's Hands

*Strength for Today,
Bright Hope for Tomorrow*

Survival for Busy Women

A Tea to Comfort Your Soul

*The Twelve Teas®
of Christmas*

*The Twelve Teas®
of Friendship*

*The Twelve Teas®
of Celebration*